HONCHO

ABHIK BHANU

Copyright © 2020 by Abhik Bhanu

All rights reserved. This book or any portion thereof may not be reproduced or transmitted in any form or manner, electronic or mechanical, including photocopying, recording, or by any information storage or retrieval system, without the express written permission of the copyright owner except for the use of brief quotations in a book review or other noncommercial uses permitted by copyright law.

Printed in the United States of America

Library of Congress Control Number: 2020921768
ISBN: Softcover   978-1-64908-514-6
        eBook   978-1-64908-513-9

Republished by: PageTurner Press and Media LLC
Publication Date: 11/03/2020

To order copies of this book, contact:

PageTurner Press and Media
Phone: 1-888-447-9651
order@pageturner.us
www.pageturner.us

HONCHO

Of the film fraternity,

For the film fraternity,

By the film fraternity.

To screenwriters and directors

CHAPTER 1

"Who is your honcho here?" Jabbar demanded loudly. Iqbal stepped up slowly and stood in front of the dreaded terrorist Jabbar Ellahi. He had a deep voice; Iqbal noticed and looked up a bit to check him out. Attractive, like a Hollywood hero, tall, dashing, blue-eyed with sharp features, long hair falling on his shoulders and a full beard on his face—these made him a complete macho. He had worn an old faded, stonewashed jeans and a long dull brown Kashmiri Phiran.

A terrorist? Yes, they are deadly. Kashmiri terrorists are good looking and noxious. They do not hesitate to kill. He may have a handsome face, but he has perilous intentions. Iqbal was thinking hard and trying to keep his cool at the same time.

"Do you know who I am?" Jabbar Ellahi asked Iqbal, gazing straight into his eyes.

Iqbal was tall, whitish, and lean. He was smart and had a fit body. He was casually dressed in a pair of blue denims and had rolled the sleeves of his black-and-white checkered shirt, half sweater, and a loose jacket thrown over it.

Iqbal shook his head slowly from left to right and right to left which meant no.

"I am the reply to your jokes that you Indians cracked when Article 370 was revoked." He smiled. "I will send one dead body to the Government of India every day." He paused and glanced at the entire movie crew. "Who is ready to die first?"

No one spoke. Absolute silence prevailed. It was a scene straight out of a movie. Except, this was not reel life, but real life. Mushtaq, skinny and agile like a monkey, turned his body left and right to watch carefully. He had short hair and an oblong face with sunken cheeks.

The movie crew was made to sit in a temporary tin shed. The terrorists were standing around them holding automatic rifles. The sun rays had faded from scarlet into grays, which were quickly getting darker. The sky was still visible, and so was the plateau covered in green grass. The abducted movie crew had lost hopes of their lives. Their silent lips prayed for mercy to the god they believed in. They feared that the terrorists wouldn't spare their lives despite their prayers. Some of the terrorists were smoking beedis, casually looking at them like they were not humans but sacrificial goats.

"We will send them the cadavers as gifts," skinny Mushtaq, his man Friday, sounded happy at the thought. He glanced at Crystal and Chandni.

Tipu, a humpty-dumpty with a little beard on his chin, smiled meaningfully at Omar. Line producer Kabir Chauhan, sitting right up front, peed in his pants. The urine flowed down his trousers.

"Cowards!" Omar, a young teenage boy with his round chubby cheeks still smooth, found it loathsome.

"You know what is the most disgraceful and disgusting thing about this film fraternity?" Jabbar turned toward Mushtaq, "They use cosmetics like women and make their faces up. How shameless they are."

"Shame! Shame! Shame!" all of them voiced their opinion in unison.

"They are *Bhands* (a community of dancers). They sing and dance. They waste time, do nothing but corrupt the culture!" Jabbar yelled. "They are fake!"

Salim, a tall half-bearded guy with a gun on his left shoulder, whispered in Jabbar's ear, "Call on the satellite phone. It's Rehman."

"Count them all," Jabbar instructed them before moving back to his den. "I will be back in a minute."

"Yes, Bhai." Mushtaq and Omar exchanged looks. Mushtaq got cold feet when he heard that he had to count them. It was a challenging task for him; he had no idea where to begin.

Abbas, who had a cruel face with strong cheekbones and a beard without mustache, gave Changez a knowing smile. He knew how bad Mushtaq's basic math was. Changez was another cruel-looking face with bucked teeth. Both Abbas and Changez were noticed by Chandni. She felt spine-chilling fear just looking at them. She shifted her gaze immediately to Crystal, who was equally terrified. They saw Jabbar getting into the den.

***

It all happened so suddenly. Before Iqbal and the crew realized what had gone wrong, they were abducted. Iqbal was trying to send messages secretly to Inspector Javed and Major Aditya from his second phone, but there wasn't any network in that area. The terrorists had confiscated their mobile phones. Iqbal managed to hide one. But it was of no use.

Iqbal was pensive. It all began two months ago. His phone rang incessantly that morning at around 11:00 AM.

CHAPTER 2

"One phone call could change your life in this industry." Batuk Anjan lit a cigarette, sucked it deeply through his fist, and released a smoke cloud from his nose. Batuk was one of the biggest agents in Bollywood. He had spent thirty-five years in the industry. He had seen many stars made out of one phone call. "Friday, he had not a single penny to survive, Monday he was a huge star." Iqbal, too, had waited for that one call for a decade. None came.

"What if there is no call?" asked Iqbal to get the reply he already knew. He was curious as to how Batuk survived all these years in Bollywood with such pathetic lines with no sales value. Iqbal was sure no one bought it coming from a tout who desperately searched for alcohol after 8:00 PM. Batuk knew all the biggies and he was clad in typical Jitendra style, white safari suit and white shoes. *Where does he get his white shoes now?*

"Some of them go back to their native places. Many just rot away or adjust to surviving somehow and a few—" He snapped his fingers to get rid of the ash on his cigarette tip.

"Few?"

"Commit suicide."

He hinted at the big production companies ruling and controlling the entertainment industry for generations.

"Nepotism?" He faked innocence.

Batuk smiled and smoked.

Iqbal had finished his three years' degree course at FTII (Film and Television Institute of India) in Pune and had come to Mumbai to become a film director. Shweta, his classmate, stood by his side. They stayed together in an apartment and worked together. Both struggled to get newer and bigger projects.

Iqbal's Samsung m20 received a call from Lalwani's office on 7 August immediately after the revocation of Article 370 from Jammu and Kashmir.

"Am I talking to Iqbal Ali?" Nayana Muke, Lalwani's manager called.

"Yes," Iqbal spoke casually.

"I am calling from Mr. Lalwani's office." The name alerted Iqbal. It might be something important. "Mr. Lalwani wanted to see you today. What time can you make it?"

"In an hour's time. I stay in Andheri."

"You have to reach Bandstand. Have you seen Arbaaz Khan's office? Right next to it."

He took a quick shower, wore his jeans and checkered shirt with folded sleeves, and used his best deodorant. Shweta had to hurry too. She put on her navy-blue torn jeans and paired it with a white top. They reached their destination before time.

They didn't have to wait. His manager Nayana Muke guided them to his huge cabin where Lalwani awaited him.

"Come, Iqbal." Lalwani was chewing fennel. He offered them a seat. His belly was bursting out of his expensive linen shirt. His fat and heavy body was cozily settled on the white couch and seemed it would never come out from that couch. He stared at Iqbal through a slit between bags and wrinkles of his eyes. *He must have a damaged liver with excessive drinking, heart problem because of tensions, diabetic? He has money and diseases.* His cabin was huge, with white walls where the frames of his movies hung. Two revolving chairs and a big throne were arranged around a round shiny glass table.

"I have seen synopsis of your story and your bio that you emailed us. You have done filmmaking course from FTII?"

When did I send him any synopsis and which one? Iqbal tried to recall. Nothing!

"Yes. Also, I have been working for ten years now. Assisted many top directors—" Iqbal wanted to rattle out an impressive list of directors, but he was interjected.

"I know." Lalwani smiled. "I am looking for a love story that can be shot in Kashmir. Do you have any?"

"I sure have one." Iqbal recalled the story now!

"Can you brief me in five minutes? Just the summary?"

Iqbal briefed him.

"Is this ready as a script? Have you written the screenplay too?"

"I have."

"Can you email us the full script?"

"Sure."

The meeting was over without any frills. It was just cut and dry business—no discussions, no hospitality. Lalwani's face was expressionless throughout. He didn't even comment on the storyline!

Both Shweta and Iqbal were disappointed with such a cold response.

"Black coffee Americano," Iqbal placed an order standing at the counter of Starbucks in Infinity Mall.

"How many?" asked the girl standing at the counter.

"Two."

Iqbal and Shweta took a corner seat. Iqbal opened his laptop and emailed the script to Lalwani. Both sipped their coffee silently. They watched people around them chatting about movie scripts and proposals. This Starbucks was full of filmy crowd.

"Let's watch a movie," Shweta broke the silence and tried to distract Iqbal.

"Okay," a mechanical reply from Iqbal. He was preoccupied and drowned in self-doubt, going over the details of the meeting in his head. *Was my narration bad? Does my story hold water?*

They bought the tickets and watched the movie *X-Men: Dark Phoenix*. The movie was over at 8: 30 PM. He walked out and looked at his phone, which was on silent mode. He saw a missed call and a WhatsApp message: "Call me back."

The call was from a new number. The true caller identified it as Lalwani.

Iqbal returned the call.

"Hello."

"Oh, Iqbal, can you come down to the office?"

"Now?"

"Yes, can you make it now?"

"Yes, I can." Iqbal looked at Shweta staring at him to know who it was.

Iqbal gave Shweta the news without too much enthusiasm or hope. They were at Lalwani's office in no time.

Nayana Muke welcomed them with a smile. "I need your full name and address."

Iqbal scribbled it on a piece of paper without asking any questions.

"Here comes the man who I waited for hours!" Financer Balram Lalwani shook hands and said. "We have decided to go ahead with your story." Lalwani was a changed man.

Iqbal couldn't believe his ears. He looked at Shweta.

"I emailed you the screenplay on Kashmir's *Azadi*," Iqbal reminded him.

Was it that one missed call that promised to change his career graph overnight? Iqbal wondered. *Is this his chance to become somebody from nobody? Is he also going to be famous?*

"You didn't mention Prabhas and Crystal know you."

"I never got a chance!" Iqbal replied politely. "I have worked with them when I was the first AD."

"I have spoken to Prabhas Venkatesh. He was looking for a script to be shot in Kashmir."

Iqbal knew Lalwani was a shrewd businessman. He understood the reason for the changed atmosphere. Prabhas and Crystal gave him a green signal.

"Kashmir government must be offering a subsidy for film shooting in Kashmir," Iqbal talked about the economic aspects of the project.

"Forget the subsidy, Iqbal. Think big. The subsidy is peanuts. My plan is to buy land there in the near future. This would be just a beginning," He sipped water. "I am planning to make a film city out there. You concentrate on the script and make a wonderful team. Money is not a problem."

Lalwani's advocate Sunil Dewan presented a ready agreement. Iqbal's name was duly mentioned as the writer and director of the film *Azadi*.

Pabst Blue Ribbon 1844 beer was served before they locked the deal. They drank the expensive $44 bottle, smoked Marlboro cigarettes, and closed the deal by signing the agreement.

"We have got Kashmir. It's a big debacle for Pakistan. We have shown the world that Pakistan can only bark. It can't do a thing," Lalwani was excited.

How is it Pakistan's debacle? Kashmir is with us already. Iqbal thought, but he didn't argue. He had learned the hard way. Never argue with rich people, especially with investors like Balram Lalwani, who had political connections.

"A star from the south in the lead role and beautiful Crystal from Bollywood," Lalwani's box office predictions were superb. "Prabhas has a good market in all four southern states—Andhra, Tamil Nadu, Kerala, and Karnataka." Crystal was a star in Bollywood. It was a perfect combination for national commercial success of the movie. Lalwani got calls from distributors when he discussed the proposal with film agents.

Iqbal and Shweta reached home and continued their celebrations with their usual Kingfisher beer and smoked Gold Flake.

***

Shweta became Iqbal's first AD, Aman was the second AD, Jackson joined as the third AD, and Nihal was the newcomer who was supposed to be the clapper boy. Rambabu-Shyambabu, the duo, was hired and contracted to serve the best food for the crew. Mastani-Mallika were the best-known choreographers. They had a team of well-trained dancers with them. They were known for their sexy figures and oversized breasts more than their dancing skills.

Chandni Mehra, fair like a Caucasian, with long hair and sharp features, was hired for costumes. Kabir joined as a line producer; he was well experienced in handling a large crew.

Iqbal worked hard and made a strong team of 371 people including all departments. The entire team was excited about shooting in Kashmir.

"It's happening!" Iqbal kissed Shweta when he was a little high that night.

"It happened." Shweta kissed back. "We need to shop. Kashmir is cold—very cold."

Iqbal agreed that they needed warm clothes.

It was a huge opportunity for Iqbal. He had worked as an assistant for nearly a decade. This was the first time he was getting a break as an independent director. He had to finish shooting at a stretch in sixty days. He was confident of achieving it. Prabhas Venkatesh had a series of meetings to understand the story and treatment with Crystal. Iqbal convinced the entire crew that Kashmir was safe now. The central and the state government both assured him. After Article 370 was revoked, J&K was a half state, governed directly by the central government. The army had full control.

The weather was cold in Kashmir, with chilly winds sneaking into bones. The first day of the shooting went without a hitch. The whole crew enjoyed a bonfire with free-flowing booze. They shook a leg to the latest Western music and some mixed tracks of Bollywood.

***

The prime minister addressed the nation immediately after 370 was revoked. He appealed to all the industries, especially film industry, to start work in the valley. Also, the state government promised Iqbal that they would take full responsibility of safety and security of the crew.

Army had deputed Major Aditya Raghuvanshi to be in charge of their security with Senior Police Inspector Javed Khan.

The party lasted almost till the crack of dawn. Major Aditya was a little tipsy; he proposed to glamorous Crystal. She smiled and asked why people proposed to her when they were drunk. Prabhas Venkatesh was engaged in taking selfies with Javed's relatives.

Everything was hunky-dory.

***

The next morning, Prabhas Venkatesh was badly hungover and highly under slept.

"I am not feeling well," He requested Iqbal, "Can you please do the scenes where I am not required?" He smoked and had black coffee but nothing worked. "I need some sleep. That's it. I will be okay by afternoon."

Iqbal decided to go ahead without him and shoot a song portion where he was not required. The next day, they shot the song till evening.

"Let's go back to the hotel. This valley gets dark quickly and could be dangerous," Major Aditya Raghuvanshi warned. They packed up and boarded their vehicles, which were escorted by two military trucks full of armed troops and two police jeeps.

Aditya Raghuvanshi's truck headed the fleet. Javed was in the middle, and the second military truck was at the tail end, protecting the movie crew. Iqbal, Crystal, Shweta, KK (Krishna Kant), Mastani-Mallika, and Chandni were traveling in the SUV. The dancers were in the vanity van. Everyone else was in the buses. Everyone was tired; some were dozing after a day's work.

They had no idea when and what happened—how Jabbar Ellahi made them hostages in the presence of military and police force.

Iqbal opened his eyes when the SUV stopped. The road was blocked. A thin man with his face covered hopped inside the SUV. He pointed a gun at the driver, "Anyone who moves will die." He meant business. Iqbal wondered if he was still dreaming, or was it for real?

CHAPTER 3

The entire Kashmir was in deep slumber except for Shabbir Mallik. He was anxiously waiting for a message. He restlessly looked at his silver iPhone time and again.

This wealthy Kashmiri politician lived alone in his lavish bungalow with Liyakat, his man Friday and Lukman, his cook. His white icy face and French beard were reminders of one of the British officers in the colonial era. He was always in black sherwani, for some reason known only to him. Maybe black suited him, or it was a show of protest to the Indian government.

His family lived in London. Shabbir was a frequent visitor to Kashmir. He was a political leader known for his searing speeches. Every politician of Kashmir was either under house arrest, detained, or watched by the military. All were crippled as the whole valley was locked down. There was nothing but an eerie silence on the streets of Kashmir. The Indian Military men, barracks, and empty roads had become Kashmir. Apple industry hit 10,000 crores loss. A government school was burnt. Shopkeepers who tried to open their shops were shot dead by terrorists. No troops could stop them. They stopped celebrating Eid in protest.

The government of the day wanted to show that Kashmir was peaceful, and business was going on as usual. Ajit Dayal successfully made a strategic effort. He called a delegation of European Union MPs to visit and assess the situation in Kashmir. The move was criticized by the media. They called them Nazi supporters and alleged that twenty-three delegates were handpicked by the prime minister. They also questioned the government that didn't allow democratically elected Indian leaders like Rahul, Yashwant, and many Indian MPs. They were detained and asked to return to Delhi. The government arrested Kashmiri leaders just like that and mocked them by inviting foreigners in. Many senior leaders had to appeal to the Supreme Court of India for permission to visit Kashmir.

The European delegations initially made a statement that Kashmir was India's internal matter. Later, German Chancellor Merkel made a statement that the Kashmir situation was unsustainable.

Shabbir was watching every single incident in Kashmir keenly. He had to plan his game, a big one, not just killing a few shopkeepers or burning schools. His friends and supporters were pressurizing him. He had to prove himself and do something spectacular. It was his showtime.

Shabbir had played his gambit. He knew what happened in the valley that night. Rehman, his confidante, was in touch with Jabbar Ellahi. Rehman was the only communication link apart from the satellite phone. He was waiting for Rehman to give him further news.

"We have got the goats. Preparing to make mutton tomorrow and distribute it to people. Thank you for your kindness and donation." Shabbir's iPhone received this message. His face lit up with a smile. He understood the meaning of the message. Work was done. Jabbar Ellahi had successfully abducted the movie crew.

"Inshallah!" he typed the message and sent it to Rehman.

Shabbir Mallik's phone rang. He shared the news with Muneer Ahmed Lonem, "Please come tomorrow early in the morning. We will have tea together." Shabbir ended the call. Liyakat and Shabbir discussed the future plan of action.

"Jabbar will send a dead body to Rehman's place. It's your responsibility to hand it over to the army," Shabbir Mallik instructed and sighed. "He will send the body tonight. We have to inform the army tomorrow early in the morning."

"It will be done. Inshallah!"

Shabbir Mallik stood and looked out through the window. The cold dark night had spread dew on the grass. It was shining like diamonds in the lamplight.

CHAPTER 4

Abduction was planned meticulously by Jabbar Ellahi and his men. Terrorists knew the terrain like the back of their hand. Military and local police were not so familiar with all the narrow lanes and hilly roads.

Skinny Mushtaq lit a bidi and announced, "Anyone tries to escape will die. The whole area is surrounded by a deep trench. There are hungry animals waiting for food. It's up to you if you fellows want to be their dinner." Mushtaq warned while he sucked the bidi and filled his lungs with smoke.

Iqbal felt a strong urge to smoke. Even a bidi was fine in the given situation, but he didn't dare ask Mushtaq for a bidi.

Mushtaq was right. The hilltop plateau did have a deep trench around it. A couple of narrow roads lead to the plateau. There were wooden platforms made on treetops where men armed with guns stood guard.

"Surrender your mobile phones." Tipu shook his heavy body, ordered, and opened a big plastic bag. Salim and Omar collected all the phones.

"Anyone with guns?" Omar asked.

"We have duplicate guns," said Fight Master Maqsood.

"Give it to us," Salim took all the toy guns.

There were temporary tin sheds made in all four corners which were covered by greenery. Iqbal noticed that there was no way out. If anyone tried to run away, he would be shot. Even if they escaped the bullet, they would fall inside the trench.

***

Jabbar Ellahi was in a den. He was looking out in the dark through a small window.

"Did you count them?" Jabbar Ellahi asked.

"They are approximately 350, I think," Mushtaq replied.

"Approximately?" Jabbar was pissed off, "You think?"

"I tried to count. They are a big crowd." He looked at Salim, Tipu, and Omar. He wasn't sure.

"Go. Count again," Jabbar commanded.

They went out and came back after a while.

Omar and Tipu's figure differed from Mushtaq's and Salim's count. Jabbar was upset.

"Can't you count the exact number of film crew? It can't be a big deal, can it? It's basic math Mushtaq."

"My counting is right," Mushtaq said confidently. "They are 355."

"Nope," Salim disagreed, "361."

"Whose count is the right one?" Jabbar was irritated.

They were weak in math. They had done it in the past too.

"Do you remember when we robbed the bank in Baramula?"

"I do."

"You couldn't count the money," Jabbar reminded them, looking into their eyes. It was a very embarrassing memory for them.

"We had to rob the same bank for currency-counting machine," he paused, "Remember?"

They were quiet.

Mushtaq, Tipu, Omar, and Salim knew what had happened.

Their math was worse. Counting this large crowd accurately was a daunting task.

"So go count them again, and this time, everyone's number should match." All of them walked out silently. Mushtaq had a silent question in his eyes, *How to count them?* The others looked at him hopefully.

Mushtaq went to the movie crew again. He saw Iqbal, Shweta, and Crystal together. An idea sparked in his head. He whistled and called Iqbal, "Hey you, filmi honcho, come here."

Iqbal walked to him.

"Do you know to count?"

"Yes. I hope so."

"We have to count the crew precisely. Exact total number! Can you count for me?"

"I know the number. The exact total number," Iqbal offered help.

"No. I do not want your number. You have to count for me." Mushtaq was adamant. "Right in front of me. Count and tell me." Mushtaq didn't want to take any chance.

"There is an easy way for it," Iqbal suggested. "Stand them in a line and ask them to count the numbers one after another. The number called by the last man is the final number."

Mushtaq liked the idea.

He yelled, "Stand in a line, make a queue, and start counting from left to that end." He showed them the last man standing. "Anyone misses the counting will be shot."

Mushtaq pointed a gun at them. Salim and Omar followed and took out their guns too. Changez wasn't sure it would work. The counting started and ended. The last man was Lightman Gagan Prasad. He counted his number 370.

***

Jabbar Ellahi came out of the den. He looked at them and heard the final number.

"Total 370 *Bhands*," Mushtaq said proudly.

"What a justice by Allah. They have revoked Article 370, and Allah has sent us 370 people to be killed and sent to them," Jabbar said loudly.

"They were actually 371. Heard of Prabhas Venkatesh, the famous actor? He was left behind," Omar showed off.

"Yes, I have seen him. He was jumping like a monkey in a video," Jabbar recalled. "So who is going to die first?" He didn't give much importance to the one that was left out.

He looked at Iqbal.

"Tell me, honcho. Who will be dying first?" Mushtaq raised his voice.

Iqbal stepped ahead and stood in front of him.

"Decide fast. Every day, one cadaver. Whose body will be sent first?" Jabbar repeated.

"I am ready to end my life," Iqbal made his point politely, "If you want to send a body, kill me first," Iqbal offered.

"Oh really!" Jabbar looked at him, "Do you think I am joking? Is this fake, like your movies, where everything is fiction and drama? I am Jabbar Ellahi. I fight for Kashmir. I am a freedom fighter." He showed him the guns his men were carrying. "These guns are real. A bullet will make a hole in your head. We have bombs, which will blow off your head from your shoulder." He chuckled and stepped towards him. "How do you want to die? With a bullet or a bomb?" Iqbal was quiet. "I am giving you a chance to choose," Jabbar offered him, "You can die later."

"They are here because of me. I brought them here," Iqbal was cool and polite, "It's my responsibility to keep them safe here."

"How can they be safe once you are dead?" Mushtaq asked.

"Let Almighty decide who dies and who lives after I die. I stand by my commitment I made to them before I left Mumbai. I can't see anyone die in front of me. They trusted me when we left for Kashmir," Iqbal looked fearless. He knew they would kill everyone anyway. But he offered his own life first.

"Okay fine! You brought them here, you die," Jabbar smiled, "You feel responsible, so die." He looked around.

"I am giving you a last chance. You can die later. Breathe for a few more days. You guys have more than a year! 370 days," Jabbar offered again.

"Yes, you can live for some time because you helped us count the exact number," Mushtaq joked. Changez and Salim laughed when Mushtaq made fun of them.

"Everyone has to die at the end of the day. Time of death is fixed by Allah," Iqbal made a serious statement, "It's in Almighty's hand."

"Enough. You are right. I agree. So die now." Jabbar made a decision to kill him first. "Get me the new rifle, which I got from Pakistan." Mushtaq went and came back with a shining new rifle.

"You have to send his body to Rehman's place. He would take it from there," Jabbar said pointing the gun at Iqbal. Iqbal was cool. He knew he would die now. He looked at Shweta. She was silent, but her cute face had turned white and stony. Tears were rolling down her face. Jabbar opened the safety latch and looked into Iqbal eyes. He was cool, ready to die.

Jabbar was flabbergasted with Iqbal's serenity. *A Bhand, who makes fictional movies and writes imaginary stories, is not afraid of death. Let him die if he wishes to.* Jabbar's middle finger crawled to the gun's trigger. He took an aim.

"Do you know this rifle? It is Barret M82, US Army designated M107. It the best sniper rifle ever made. It will rip off your head and go through a hundred heads. It will pierce brick and stone."

All 369 crew members stood shocked, holding their breath. They saw daring Iqbal standing there, ready to embrace death. They were sad and worried. If Iqbal died, there would be no one left to save them.

"Let me tell you one thing before you die. You are lucky that you will be shot with the best rifle ever made in this world. It is a wonderful piece of technology," Jabbar kept boasting, "I can kill you with a revolver, but I want to respect your death as you have offered yourself first."

Jabbar pointed the rifle again at Iqbal. Iqbal stood with his eyes closed, waiting for death.

Jabbar pulled the trigger. Everyone heard the click of the rifle. There was no bullet in the rifle. Mushtaq realized his mistake. He had forgotten to load the magazine.

Iqbal thought he was dead when he heard the click. Beads of sweat appeared on his forehead in the chilly climate. Then he opened his eyes. He saw Jabbar looking at him. *Am I alive?* He asked himself. He was relieved with the answer. *Yes, I am alive.*

"Bhai, just wait. Give me the rifle. I will load it now. It was a new gun, and I was hasty," Mushtaq was apologetic. Jabbar was silent. No one spoke. Everyone waited for Jabbar's next move. Jabbar headed back to his den quietly. Mushtaq, Omar, and Salim followed him into the den.

CHAPTER 5

India Pride Hotel, Srinagar.

Prabhas Venkatesh slept all day. He felt heavy headed when he woke up. He had skipped lunch and had just black coffee late in the afternoon. He had an early, light dinner and walked on the hotel's lawn to get some fresh air. He sat down alone for some time. It felt good. He loved his rare solitude. He liked the cool breeze. He was feeling a lot better now. He should be able to shoot tomorrow.

Prabhas noticed a pretty girl in tight blue jeans and a black jacket staring at him from the lobby. He knew she was a journalist. She would chew his brain. He wasn't in any mood to give her an interview.

Why was the unit not back yet? He wondered and tried calling Crystal, Iqbal and some others from the crew. No one responded. All phones were switched off. Hotel owner Sukhvinder Singh walked in and politely asked if he could talk. He certainly didn't want to invade the privacy of his VIP guest.

"May I disturb you for a moment?"

"Oh! Come on. Don't be so formal." Prabhas welcomed him warmly, "In fact I was getting bored alone."

Sukhvinder and Prabhas chatted for some time.

"I have renovated this hotel after Article 370 was revoked." Sukhvinder said.

"It's a wonderful place." Prabhas was polite.

"This girl is a big fan of yours. She has waited the whole day for an interview with you. Her name is Ayesha Alam." Sukhvinder pointed towards the lobby.

Prabhas wasn't in any mood to face a journalist. But they were an occupational hazard. He smiled.

"Okay, call her. I will give her some time. Just a light chat." He chuckled, "Anything for you Papaji."

***

Ayesha was called inside his hotel suite.

"Hi, I am Ayesha Alam from Valley News channel." Ayesha entered and introduced herself.

Prabhas Venkatesh smiled in response and placed an order for a pot of coffee. He sat on the reclining chair in the middle of the room. Ayesha had switched on her mobile camera Samsung Galaxy S20 Ultra to capture him.

"Ready Sir?" Ayesha asked politely. She knew it was important for her career. Her editor Rudra Shekhar would definitely pat her back for this exclusive interview. Prabhas Venkatesh was cool and relaxed. He knew there would be questions about his life. Same boring stuff, 'What do you think of the story of the film? Tell us about it.' 'How do you like Kashmir?' 'How do you inspire the youth of the nation?' and may be a couple of personal questions, 'What do you do in your spare time? Or what's your favorite food?'

***

Army headquarters.

Major Aditya Raghuvanshi and senior police inspector Javed Khan were standing in front of general Jang Bahadur.

"You mean, all those vehicles just vanished?"

"We couldn't understand Sir." Aditya Raghuvanshi was nervous and sheepish.

"When did you realize?"

"Our vehicles were together in a convoy, but we found their vehicles missing when we stopped to pee." Aditya spoke like a loser.

"Where are the two film stars, Prabhas Venkatesh and Crystal?" General asked.

"Prabhas is in the hotel. He skipped the shoot today. He was unwell. Crystal is with them."

"Go search for them." Jang Bahadur said harshly, "Increase the security at the hotel."

***

Chanakyapuri, New Delhi.

Ajit Dayal, national security adviser's personal number rang incessantly. He saw the name and took the call. It was army chief Jang Bahadur informing him about the situation.

"The entire movie crew is missing."

"Missing? What do mean?"

"They were returning to the hotel after shooting outdoors. Major Aditya and Javed found them absconding when they stopped their vehicles to check." Jang Bahadur changed the statement from 'pee' to 'check' smartly.

"You mean the entire crew has gone with their ..."

"Yes, that is what is surprising for us," Jang Bahadur interjected, "Good news is that film Star Prabhas Venkatesh is safe because he didn't go for the shoot."

"Any other famous artists in the crew?" Ajit Dayal tried to understand the situation. "Crystal was with the crew when they…"

"They? Who is 'they'?" Ajit Dayal was known for his intellect. He played a great role in Indian politics without fighting a single election.

"The terrorists I guess." Jang Bahadur speculated, "Army units are patrolling the whole valley with police teams to get any clues."

No one spoke for a moment.

"Are you sure it's the terrorists?" Dayal asked. He knew it was bad news for all. It would affect their Kashmir mission.

"Could there be an accident or a simple case of losing their way? There is no confirmed news as to what actually happened."

Accident? Lost? Ajit Dayal didn't buy it. He didn't live in a fool's paradise, he accepted truth in life no matter how hard it was.

"I mean, where could they go?" General was hesitant and confused.

"Hmm." Ajit had just finished his drink and dinner. He was about to sleep. He called and shared the news with home minister Amit Singh Thakur.

"We have to wait for the confirmation from the army about the missing film crew."

"Ensure Prabhas Venkatesh's security," home minister was concerned that media will blow up the issue beyond repairs, "Shift this guy to Delhi or Mumbai in full security ASAP."

"Yes Sir," Dayal agreed.

"What about the media?" Amit Singh Thakur pointed out the biggest problem, "Watch out."

"Hmm." Ajit Dayal knew whom to call. He disconnected the phone and called the hotel owner and inquired about the media.

"A film reporter is here." Sukhvinder informed.

"Call it off immediately. No media. Seal the hotel. I have asked army for more security." Ajit Dayal instructed.

"Yes Sir."

"Do it coolly, no one should feel that anything is wrong," Dayal cautioned him, "Go slow, don't panic."

What was wrong? Sukhvinder thought. He didn't wish to interrupt the interview between Ayesha and Prabhas.

Ajit made the next call to the army officer Ajay Duggal who was on hotel security duty.

"No one should enter the hotel without proper checking. Make sure those who enter, have some legitimate business with the hotel.

No one else. Seal the hotel, and call for more force." Ajit Dayal instructed him.

He called Rudra Shekhar, Valley News editor in chief, "Do not broadcast any story," Ajit said firmly, "No story will leak unless I say so. Hold it. I will tell you when to break it."

Shekhar knew something was fishy. Something had happened which he didn't know. Rahim came running into the cabin. Valley News was the most popular global media network based in Srinagar.

"I have an explosive." Rahim was excited, "The movie crew who was shooting here, has been abducted by terrorist Jabbar Ellahi." He finished in one breath. Shekhar offered him water.

"Source?" Shekhar asked. He had already received a call with instructions to hold.

"Very reliable army source. Aditya and Javed are with the search party." Rahim revealed.

"Wait. Let me confirm." Shekhar held the breaking story.

Rudra Shekhar took out Gold flake cigarette packet, picked two, pulled it out a bit and offered one to Rahim. He lit his cigarette and handed a lighter to Rahim. Pushed the bell. Nasim, the office boy appeared at the cabin door.

"Two black coffees." Nasim left. Both headed to the open space attached to the Shekhar's cabin. That was their smoking zone.

Rahim watched Shekhar puffing away. Rahim recognized a situation when Shekhar offered smokes and black coffee. They watched the white snow gently falling on the Chinar, sipped the coffee and enjoyed a quiet moment in the frosty weather.

***

Ayesha was busy asking questions, unaware of the developments taking place outside, "We have seen you mingling with the army and donate a huge amount to them. Even the Prime Minister has appreciated your work." Prabhas Venkatesh frowned, this Kashmiri girl asked a very unexpected question. She looked young but her question was more like a seasoned journalist.

"Yes, our soldiers work hard on the borders for the security of our country. My heart goes out to them. They are the real heroes, not us. They work under impossible conditions." Prabhas Venkatesh had explained it many times to media. He simply had to repeat it.

"Isn't it true that it has given you immense publicity and helped you build your image as a philanthropist and a patriotic actor. The audience was more positively inclined towards you and your films are now far more successful than earlier?" Ayesha paused, "Your PR activities have been doubled."

That shocked Prabhas Venkatesh. His face paled and he tensed up. *How dare she! A worthless nobody, a new comer asks me all this? Who is she?*

"Can I come back from the washroom? Stop the camera for a second." Prabhas Venkatesh tried to stand and remove the mike himself. Ayesha helped him take it off. He stepped out of his suite and walked briskly into the corridor. Ayesha realized that he was not happy with her. She waited for him anyway.

Prabhas Venkatesh reached the reception and asked for Sukhvinder Singh rudely.

"Please have a seat Sir!" the receptionist requested him politely. Sukhvinder Singh was called. "Who is this reporter? She is talking rubbish. I was ready to give her an interview on your request, but she is crossing the line, asking political questions. I am an artist, not a politician. She is pointing fingers at me claiming that I use the army for publicity."

"I will tell her to leave right away. There is some development anyway I want to talk to you about."

***

Prabhas Venkatesh turned his head to see a fleet of army vehicles heading towards the hotel. He thought the film crew had returned. He stopped to see the military trucks surrounding the hotel. Something was wrong.

Sukhvinder Singh read his thoughts and hurriedly said, "You need to be inside sir."

"Is something wrong?" he asked.

"I have been instructed to protect you."

"Where is Aditya Raghuvanshi and Javed Khan?"

"They will be here soon." Prabhas got no clear reply. He suspected danger round the corner. The film crew had not come back. There was no sign of Aditya and Javed. Something was wrong, *What? Did Pakistan attack?*

He saw Ayesha Alam packing her stuff when he entered his suite.

CHAPTER 6

Ayesha Alam entered the office. Rudra Shekhar had called her immediately. He was well informed about the interview.

"There is no need for the story now." Rudra Shekhar was firm, "There are some political developments taking place. I have asked Rahim to do the story."

"I know, extra army was called in for his security. That's why Prabhas didn't give me a full interview."

Shekhar looked at her. She was an idiot. These girls wanted to be famous journalists overnight! She had made a star angry. She didn't know what questions to ask a film star. She was a film journalist at the end of the day. Why did she ask stupid political questions? He had to take the heat from Sukhvinder. He was upset but this was not the time to discuss that.

"Who she thinks she is?" Sukhvinder was pissed off when he called.

"I will talk to her." Shekhar had to calm him down, "This wouldn't happen again, I assure you."

"Again? Ask her not to enter my hotel premise again. You have no idea how Prabhas was enraged."

Had she no idea who Prabhas was? Prabhas could have sued the news channel if he had made a few calls. All the investors would have backed out from the news channel if Prabhas would have taken some action. He was well connected in political circles. Big journalists dared not speak against him. She was a small-time reporter waiting for a scoop to get her in the lime light.

Ayesha wasn't happy. Even if it was a political story why could she not handle it. Why Rahim? She was upset.

"Shekhar I want to do this story. I know something is cooking there. It's a big breaking story." She was excited.

"Share it with Rahim Akhtar if you know anything."

"I would like to break the story." Said Ayesha.

Shekhar didn't like her attitude.

"Why don't you partner with Rahim. You two can do the story. You know he does crime and politics. We can't shift you independently in crime and politics." Shekhar lit a cigarette and suggested. Ayesha agreed. She hated movie reporting. It was a good beginning with Rahim.

***

Rahim checked Ayesha out. She was a pretty girl. Oval fair face with a pointed nose and a good figure. This filmy reporter with no previous experience, wanted to report politics with him.

"She wanted to work on a lead about the movie star Prabhas Venkatesh and the army," Shekhar briefed him, "We have to investigate the story and hold it till I ask you to break. Ayesha is naïve. Keep a watch on her. Make sure she isn't talking to media competitors. Handle her with care." Shekhar prepared Rahim thoroughly. He consoled Rahim who was busy looking for his cigarette, "You don't have to listen to her. She is not your partner. She will assist you. Remember, and I repeat! Break the story only when I tell you to." Shekhar was firm on that. Rahim realised Shekhar wanted him to understand the situation and handle it carefully.

Rahim lit the cigarette when he found one. He knew he was a cog in the wheel. Rudra couldn't do anything because he had bosses watching him. At the end of the day it's all business, everyone looked for profit.

***

7, Race Course Road, New Delhi.

The Prime Minister heard the news. Ajit Dayal briefed him, "The film crew is missing. General just informed me. A terrorist Jabbar Ellahi could have abducted them. I will reach there as soon as possible."

"Okay." PM was brief.

Missing? What did he say? Terrorist Jabbar Ellahi might have ... The PM was upset with the news to state the least.

The Home Minister, his close aide, was rushing to meet the PM. He walked out of his bungalow, on to the lawn. The security found this unusual.

PM was standing alone staring at a lamp post.

He had been fighting against terrorism for a long time now. He wanted it abolished from its roots. These Pakistanis were shameless. They never learnt to live in peace. They were raising terrorists like a crop. Jabbar Ellahi was a top Kashmiri terrorist. Young blood provoked by Pakistan in the name of radical Islam, promising them heaven full of virgins. He was tough with them. He isolated them globally but they were thick-skinned and sticky. Even after a series of wars and surgical strikes they were not ready to bow down.

Kashmir had been governed by military. International community started raising concerns about human rights.

CHAPTER 7

Jabbar Ellahi's den.

Jabbar Ellahi was in a deep thought.

This guy is fearless. How come he isn't scared of death? I have never seen anyone who is not afraid of death. Jabbar was thinking about Iqbal. Mushtaq looked at him all confused.

"Call him," Jabbar said without looking at him, "He should be on our side. He doesn't know his goal. He would be a good freedom fighter."

Mushtaq went out to fetch Iqbal.

"Hey, you honcho. Come here. Bhai is calling you." Mushtaq whistled and ordered.

Iqbal got up and walked with Mushtaq towards the den. He entered it and looked around. There were a few rocks which doubled up as seats. There were series of rifles, guns, arms and ammunition arranged neatly. There were wooden boxes kept in a corner. A satellite phone was lying on the bed. Jabbar was filling weed in a white rectangular paper. He stuffed weed and rolled it in a cigarette like an expert. He looked for a matchbox. It was in his side pocket. He took it out and lit the rolled joint. He took a deep drag and sighed. Iqbal knew that peculiar smell well. He loved it too. In fact, he badly needed a drag himself. Jabbar looked at him.

"What's your name?" Jabbar asked.

"Iqbal Ali." Iqbal replied. *Why didn't he attempt for the second time, with a loaded gun? What is his plan?*

"Muslim!" Jabbar exclaimed and pulled another puff.

"I knew it," Jabbar was satisfied, "Only a Muslim has the guts and fearlessness." He touched Iqbal's shoulder, "Brother why are you doing such filthy work? This is not for you. You are brave. You are born to serve Islam."

"True. You are right. I am doing so." Iqbal agreed with him.

"You don't understand. I am talking about this filmmaking business. It's bad. Not for us." Jabbar explained.

Iqbal was quiet; his mind working at lightning speed. He looked longingly at the hand rolled joint in Jabbar's hand.

"Can I have one?"

Jabbar and Mushtaq exchanged looks and smiled. Jabbar passed his joint to him. He felt blissful as the marijuana filled his lungs. They looked at him.

"You smoke this?" Jabbar asked.

"Weed is very common in our industry." Iqbal was smoking as if he was with his friends sharing a joint at a party. He was fearless.

Jabbar continued the conversation again. "You have to quit movie making business and join us with your crew."

"Hmm" Iqbal smoked more. Mushtaq was little pissed off.

"Kashmir's freedom is our purpose." Jabbar stressed on 'freedom'.

Mushtaq jumped the gun, "Are you getting what Bhai is trying to make you understand?" He was loud and aggressive.

"I am." Iqbal assured him. He kept his cool and continued smoking.

"Be with us. Fight for Kashmir. Join us." Mushtaq invited him.

"I am doing the same thing. You are doing it directly and my way is indirect. I am fighting for freedom as are you. We both are on the same side." Iqbal explained. Jabbar finished his joint but continued listening.

"This government is trying to abolish the very culture of Kashmir. Kashmiris are Allah's people. They are blessed with extraordinary beauty and wonderful traditions." Iqbal stopped to see their faces, he continued smoking. They were happy to hear him praise Kashmir as 'Allah's people'. "This film will be forever. Generation after generation will watch their culture and enjoy the love story and Kashmir's freedom struggle." Iqbal had finished smoking his joint and felt good.

"Freedom?" Mushtaq was surprised, "Is it a freedom story?"

"It is. The protagonist comes from London and falls in love with a Kashmiri girl."

"It's a love story."

"The government will not let me make the movie, if I directly make it a freedom story. But it is mainly a freedom story. Do you know the name of the movie?"

They looked at each other puzzled.

"*Azadi.*" Iqbal replied proudly.

They were doubtful and silent.

"You are lying." Mushtaq was direct. He looked into Iqbal's eyeballs.

"No, I am not. Check if you don't trust me. Call anyone from the film unit and ask them. You will know if I am telling you the truth!" Iqbal countered immediately.

Mushtaq looked at Salim and insinuated he find out the name of the movie from the crew. Jabbar, Mushtaq, Omar waited for Salim to crosscheck and come back.

Iqbal sat on a big stone kept in the corner. Mushtaq didn't like this. *Had he forgotten his limits? He asked for weed! I smoke bidis and never dared to ask for a joint. It was Jabbar's prerogative. It's expensive! Look at this guy. Had the weed affected his mind? How dare he sit in front of Jabbar?* He slapped him tight.

"How dare you sit in front of Bhai without permission?"

"Sorry." Iqbal got up quickly.

"It's okay. You may sit." Jabbar allowed him to be seated.

Iqbal decided to keep standing.

Salim came back with information, "*Azadi* is really the name of the movie." Iqbal was right.

Jabbar Ellahi knew Iqbal was trustworthy. He could be used. They had another connection now, a 'weed' connection. Iqbal had a smile on his lips. Jabbar's confidence doubled. He had a proposal ready for Iqbal.

"Iqbal your team is strong 370, right?" Jabbar was cool when he said that.

"Yes Bhai." Iqbal replied politely.

"We are forty-two in total. We were seventy-five but our friends died in army and police operations after they abolished Article 370." Jabbar paused, looked down, and continued after a while, "They killed my closest friend Arman."

Mushtaq, Salim, Omar felt sad too. Iqbal finished smoking.

"We will make a strong gang if you all come with us." Jabbar tried to sound normal when he said that, "We would be forty-two plus 370, a good number in total."

Jabbar tried to calculate. He looked at Omar. He knew Mushtaq was no good at math. Iqbal understood they were calculating as he saw Omar pretending to count on his fingers. Mushtaq looked at Salim. Jabbar finally looked at Iqbal.

"Four hundred and twelve." Iqbal added quickly, "Four hundred twelve total number. We are with you Bhai. All of us. It's one team." Iqbal replied positively.

"Let's fight for Kashmir. Find out from the team who is ready to blow himself against the army. Let's plan and send men inside the camp." Jabbar wanted it quick.

"We are fighting for Kashmir. Saving its legacy; it is known for Persian as well as Central Asian culture which is dying."

"You said that Iqbal. Bhai isn't talking about that. We want freedom," Mushtaq was irritated, "Remember you would have gone to Allah if the gun was loaded."

"I would have thanked Bhai if I would have gone to Allah," Iqbal was polite and sincere.

"You would have thanked me?" Jabbar was surprised. *Has he gone mad? What is he saying?*

"Yes, Bhai I was trying to be famous for over a decade. You have done it by abducting us. The entire world knows by now that we are hostages. All television channels worldwide must be debating my movie '*Azadi*' & me. My name and picture would be on the front page of every newspaper nationally & internationally.

All social media must be making fake and real stories about me. You made me immortal. My movie is a big hit before it is made," Iqbal spoke extempore.

He has a point. Jabbar thought, *what he said was right.*

"Also, you made a great decision by keeping us alive and not killing us." Iqbal started again. Jabbar was now interested in Iqbal's point of view.

Mushtaq stared at him. Iqbal took a long pause to assess their reactions. Mushtaq gave him a hard look. He knew Iqbal would come with some new angle. Iqbal was trying to be over smart, he thought. But Jabbar was interested to know, why 'not killing Iqbal' was a great decision.

"Okay, why was it a good decision?" Iqbal had made Jabbar curious. He enjoyed the conversation.

"Army & police would wait for you to take action. They have to follow orders from the politicians in power, right?" He looked at Jabbar and continued, "Politicians are answerable to people and media. Media would ask tough questions and pressurize them to take action. They will have no valid reason to take any action unless you send a dead body to them. Once they get a body, they would order the army for an extensive search operation with helicopters."

"They can't come here." Mushtaq made his point and discarded Iqbal's logic. "This place is between India and Pakistan. Helicopters would be shot down in this air space."

"That's exactly my point." Iqbal said excitedly, "If an Indian helicopter gets shot, then there will be war. It will be on us. Everyone will be killed. Later, the politicians would say it was in retaliation." Iqbal sighed, "The present government will not think twice and this situation will justify their war with Pakistan."

"We are not scared of war." Omar said.

"But that is not what you want, do you? Your purpose is Kashmir's freedom." Iqbal was quick to reply.

"Okay! So, what is the right step according to you?" Jabbar was asking for a suggestion from Iqbal.

"Corner government of India with a threat that you will kill all 370 persons of the movie crew if Article 370 is not reinstated in Kashmir. That would create a havoc in the world and the government would be forced to comply with your demand. They would be under pressure." Iqbal sighed and looked at Jabbar.

"You have a point. Let's negotiate with the Government of India to reinstate article 370 or we will kill 370 film crew members." Jabbar accepted Iqbal's idea.

"Total international community will talk about you." Iqbal added to drive the point home, "Media will broadcast and discuss Kashmir's problem and injustice done to Kashmiris. They would know that article 370 revocation was undemocratic."

"Hmm." Jabbar scratched his beard and agreed with Iqbal.

Iqbal realized he had the Big Boss on his side. He was now worried about his crew members who had not eaten anything after lunch.

"Can we have dinner? We have very good cooks, Rambabu and Shyambabu. They make delicious food." Iqbal made an offer which no one could reject." Mushtaq looked at Jabbar. He nodded his head in approval.

"That can be allowed. Rambabu Shyambabu can cook. But Iqbal always remember, I appreciate people who are smart. People who act over smart- I kill them. Never ever try to be over smart with me." Jabbar warned him. Everyone looked forward to a decent meal.

CHAPTER 8

Aditya Raghuvanshi came to the India Pride Hotel after a massive search operation. Five hours of patrolling ended without any positive results. Prabhas Venkatesh had left for Mumbai already.

***

The PMO checked with Ajit Dayal. There was no communication from the terrorists' side. By now they were sure it was a terrorist act. They were worried of the consequences of killing of the entire film crew. They knew they could do nothing immediately.

Intelligence Bureau and RAW (Research and Analysis Wing) were busy digging information which might help them find the exact location of the hide out. They had some idea of their whereabouts, but it was too risky to move to that location.

***

Rudra Shekhar's phone rang. He saw the name AD. He kept the coffee cup aside and picked it up without a moment's delay. Ajit Dayal was on the line. He briefed him.

Dayal instructed Mayank, "Talk of the disappearance and ask the news anchor to speculate about the plight of the movie crew. The vehicles could have met with an accident or lost their way - What would have happened? When and where it would have happened? How it could have happened?"

Dayal wanted countrymen to hear the accident news first so that they kept guessing and got confused by the time the news of abduction came out.

He further instructed Mayank, "It's sensitive. So, please handle with care."

Shekhar called the anchor Mehek Azmi and gave her the piece of paper to be read in the Breaking News section.

Shekhar called Rahim, "Leave for Mumbai and get all the details of the movie project - '*Azadi*'. Talk to all the concerned parties. Take Ayesha with you."

Shekhar knew the film crew had been abducted. He needed a follow up story.

CHAPTER 9

Rambabu and Shyambabu cooked for everyone. All of them were starving. They ate heartily and thanked the duo. There were huge iron rods over a pit in which fire was burning. There was a series of big utensils kept to cook food. This place was warm and everyone wanted a bit of the warmth to fight the cold weather.

The entire movie unit felt hugely relieved. Their faith in Iqbal doubled. He was ready to die for them and by doing so he saved all. He was a great guy. It was an emotional moment for all.

Shweta hugged Iqbal. Next were Crystal, Mastani and Mallika.

"You smoked weed?" Shweta whispered.

"Jabbar offered; I couldn't refuse." Iqbal whispered dramatically repeating famous Hollywood movie *God Father's* line.

"How could you smoke alone?" Shweta looked in to his eyes and smiled, "Next time don't forget me." Iqbal knew what she meant.

Iqbal assured everyone, "No one will die here; we are here to live. Do not be scared. Be friendly with them. They can't kill you, once you are friends with them." He looked at everyone.

"Make friends with them?" Crystal frowned.

"Yes, that's the only way out. Remember that story where a hunter helped the lion who was hurt by a thorn. The lion was in immense pain. The hunter took out the thorn and applied some lotion on the lion's paw. The lion was relieved of the pain. Few months later the king got angry with that hunter because he dared to love his daughter," Iqbal sighed and continued, "The hunter was thrown in a lion's cage. The hungry lion didn't kill the hunter because it was the same lion the hunter had helped. The king was shocked to see a hungry lion licking the hunter's face."

Iqbal paused and said, "A lion felt love and gratitude and wouldn't kill someone who helped him in distress. They are after all, human beings. They can't kill us once they get emotionally attached to us."

"Yes, I have seen a video on social media where many lions were playing with a man like he was one of them." Crystal added.

"Make friends with them." Iqbal instilled a new hope in the hearts of his crew. He motivated everyone. He knew they had lost hope and were scared for their lives. The tension was abating slowly.

***

Mushtaq and his friends had a delightful dinner after a long time. They took out bidis and smoked after dinner. They asked Rambabu, Shyambabu to make preparations for breakfast next morning.

Jabbar called his men in the den in separate groups of five and discussed what was to be done. He consulted almost everyone. He heard their suggestions without any reaction.

They were on the same page. They voiced that killing & sending one body could cause problems.

Sending a message and negotiating with the Indian Government was okay for the time being.

They wanted to see how the entire world takes it.

Mushtaq, Salim, Omar and Tipu had a bizarre advice.

"Let them be engaged with shooting and cooking food for us. We haven't seen shooting." Mushtaq said.

Jabbar Ellahi didn't want to allow them to shoot.

"Do you know it is against Islam?" Jabbar cautioned his men.

"I believe this is all Allah's wish. Allah had sent them with a certain plan," Mushtaq replied politely.

"Allah planned to start shooting here? Have you gone nuts Mushtaq?" Jabbar was irritated.

"We have to pull them on our side. We have to run with the bull if we have to stop and control the bull." Mushtaq added to prove his point.

"Muslims would join us for sure." Tipu said.

"We would kill all Hindus who refuse to be with us," Omar had deadly plans.

"They will join us. They don't have any other option. Join or die." Mushtaq said with complete determination.

It wasn't that simple, Jabbar knew it.

"We will see it in the morning." Jabbar wasn't in any haste to take the decision. He wanted to sleep over the problem.

***

"How was the food?" Iqbal asked Mushtaq.

"Not bad." Mushtaq was being a miser with his compliments. Iqbal knew that. Mushtaq didn't want to appreciate his cooks. He lit a bidi. He offered one to Iqbal.

He refused it politely, "Thank you"

"Why? You want Bhai's brand only?" "Okay give me one," Iqbal took a bidi, lit it and smoked. "Your work was brilliant."

"What work?"

"The way you kidnapped all of us with our vehicles. This is not an easy task. Especially when we had army and police guarding us."

"It was all planned, military trucks were running ahead, followed by buses and SUVs. We knew vehicles would stop at the turning. We had already placed wooden logs, wired beneath; we pulled the whole bus to the tree top with the help of the wire once it stopped at the turning." Mushtaq was bursting with pride, "We let the military trucks pass one after another."

"Hmm. Brilliant!" Iqbal appreciated, "Well planned. Just like a Hollywood film. So all the vehicles were pulled on to the tree top with wires?"

"No Iqbal. Are you an idiot? Only buses which are big had to stop at the turning. We diverted the SUVs. We had a diversion sign board ready with 'ROAD CLOSED. USE DIVERSION'. We fixed it when SUVs came. The drivers were new. We know these forest roads, they don't. We just pulled the sign board off after your vehicles were diverted and let the army and police jeeps pass."

It was a brilliant. The roads were all turns and bends and thick forest around. They couldn't see the other vehicles. The army and police went straight and movie unit's buses were pulled off. SUVs diverted to unknown locations. No one was hurt. Not a single gunshot. A movie crew of 371 with their vanity van, buses, SUVs were taken in their custody in a jiffy.

"Wow!" Iqbal was genuinely impressed by their modus operandi.

Iqbal and Mushtaq talked till late night under the temporary tin shed. Mushtaq explained it was impossible to locate them. There was no mobile network. Only satellite phone worked there.

"The route to this place is impossible to pass. It is narrow and only expert drivers well versed with the route could drive on it. Even if someone tried to drive down, they would face snags as tree branches were spread across the road blocking the access."

"Oh ...!" Iqbal was curious to know, "How did you come then?"

"We pulled the branches up with a rope. We carry long ropes with us." Mushtaq explained, "But even if anyone crossed the tree trunks, they would find a big rock in the middle of the road."

"Rock?"

"Yes, rock! Big rock." Mushtaq smiled, "Those rocks are artificial. They look gigantic."

"Hmm." Iqbal waited for Mushtaq to explain how the rocks were removed.

"The rocks are actually wooden; painted gray brown so it looks like a rock. If you tried to move it, it wouldn't budge. Because it is fixed by clamps and screws. We open it with screw drivers, push it aside and move ahead. Fix it again once our vehicles pass. Others cannot even imagine removing that rock." Mushtaq was brimming with pride.

Mushtaq pointed to the tree top and asked, "Do you see that?"

There were platforms made. Iqbal saw men with guns watching all four corners.

"Anyone tries to run away would be shot dead immediately." Mushtaq showed them, "On all four sides." Iqbal turned his neck and looked around him. Men with guns were watching them cautiously. Even if anyone tried to run, he would reach nowhere. Only they knew their exact location.

"Excellent security management." Iqbal praised, "Even a bird can't fly without your permission."

Mushtaq and Iqbal were sitting on a big rock. Mushtaq saw Chandni, Mallika, Mastani, Shweta and Crystal sitting nervously. Iqbal noticed Mushtaq eyeing the girls.

"How do you do the shooting?" Mushtaq asked when he realized Iqbal had caught him staring at the girls.

Iqbal didn't know how to explain that. He just coughed.

"Tell me, do you have a good time with them, I mean these girls are beautiful." Mushtaq smiled, "I never watched any shooting."

They had hardly seen any woman for months and here they were, living with gorgeous damsels. This close proximity with women was a bit distracting for them. Iqbal knew they were sick and tired of stressful life. They needed a break badly. They wanted some good food and relaxation.

"Do you want to watch a film shoot?" Iqbal smiled too. Mushtaq was quiet. Iqbal took it as yes. He knew Mushtaq wasn't the decision maker but he was the only one who could influence the decision. He was second in command.

Iqbal and Mushtaq had a long conversation till late night. They smoked one bidi after another.

Mushtaq had eyes only for Chandni. She had a mesmerizing smile. She had stolen his heart the first time he saw her. He would get a chance to talk to her the next day during the shooting. Their eyes met many times when he eyed her. He had decided he would save her come what may. He didn't like her downcast eyes.

The night was breaking in to dawn.

Chandni gazed at him steadily for a long time. It was a full moon that night. She opened her hair tied in ribbons and bows, inviting him to go head. "Make friends, they would never kill you." Chandni was following Iqbal's advice.

***

Shabbir Mallik woke up and looked at the watch- it was 4.00AM.

Muneer Ahmed Lone entered coughing.

"Is he sleeping?" Muneer asked Liyakat hoping that he would wake Shabbir up. He sat down and asked Liyakat to get a cup of coffee.

Shabbir Mallik came out and sat beside him on the soft spongy couch.

"Neither a cadaver nor any news. Everything is ice cold." Lone was disappointed. "Why hasn't he sent the body?" Muneer Ahmed asked Shabbir Mallik. Mallik was pensive. He didn't have answers to Muneer's questions.

"Television news is speculating an accident!" Muneer said sipping the hot coffee. Muneer was an old man in his late seventies. He felt cold. His hand trembled when he lifted the coffee mug. He looked very weak and skinny.

"Why can't we call him?" Muneer Ahmed wanted him to talk to Jabbar on the satellite phone.

"We can call him. I will call him right away."

Muneer and Shabbir were old associates. Both wanted Kashmir separated from India. Muneer's family had a flourishing leather business in United Kingdom. All his seven sons and grandsons were in flourishing leather business. Their factories in Pakistan and Afghanistan were minting money. Muneer continued to live in Kashmir as he loved it. His sons and grandsons sent money to continue the fight for Kashmir's freedom. Muneer was one of the main financial investors in the freedom movement.

Five of Muneer's men were killed by the army recently. He couldn't move out as his passport was confiscated by the state police.

***

The satellite phone ring woke Jabbar Ellahi up. Jabbar knew who was at the other end.

Jabbar called Mushtaq loudly, "Come take the call."

"Must be Shabbir Bhai," Mushtaq hurried in.

"Hmm." He was pensive. He rubbed his itchy beard. He didn't know how to handle it.

"Let me talk to him." Mushtaq said.

Jabbar knew Mushtaq would come out with some ideas. He knew his best man had great skills. He took out the weed packet and started rolling a joint.

"Hello!" Mushtaq greeted Shabbir quickly, "Assalam walekum Shabbir Bhai."

"Walekum Assalam. Is this Mushtaq? Brother, where is Jabbar?" Shabbir recognized his voice.

Jabbar had no idea how was he going to tackle it. He knew Mushtaq was smart and would come up with something.

His right hand was still on his beard.

"Bhai isn't well." Mushtaq winked at Jabbar.

"What happened to him?" Mushtaq knew this question would pop up.

"Dysentery." Mushtaq replied suddenly.

Jabbar was about to laugh.

A few moments passed in silence. Jabbar had to struggle to stop himself from laughing. He stopped smoking.

"He is running to the toilet all the time." Mushtaq added.

"Ask him to take some medicine."

"He took Lomotil. But the tablets were way past the expiration date. I don't know what to do. I will ask him to call as soon as he gets better," Mushtaq paused, "Do you want to convey any message to him?"

"No. It's okay. Ask him to talk to me." Shabbir hung up.

Mushtaq looked at Jabbar and chuckled. They both laughed heartily.

Shabbir kept the satellite phone aside.

"He is not well," Shabbir said but he looked unconvinced.

"What happened to him? Is he all right?"

"Dysentery." Shabbir looked down and saw his own reflection in the polished marble floor. "Dysentery?" Muneer Ahmed Lone repeated.

Both exchanged puzzled looks.

CHAPTER 10

Jabbar Ellahi got up and headed out of his den.

He saw Iqbal and many of his film crew members offering namaz (prayers) in the morning.

They are religious. They would join us for sure. Allah has sent them for us. Nothing happens without Allah's wish. Not a single leaf moves without his wish. He thought. Mushtaq joined him. Everyone offered namaz.

The breakfast was ready.

The spot boys Guddu, Babloo, Rafee and Pankaj served them yummy scrambled eggs with deep-fried bread and sauces.

"Iqbal was asking for permission to shoot."

"Iqbal or you?" Jabbar gave him a hard look. He knew last night Mushtaq was with Iqbal.

"It's not me alone, everyone wants to watch," Mushtaq justified, "We risk our lives, live under stress, eat half-cooked, tasteless food. This is the time Allah has sent us some relief through them. Let them jump and dance for the time being. The monkey dance will be over soon. They would join us anyway at the end of the day. Where would they go? There is no option available to them." Jabbar heard Mushtaq quietly. Mushtaq had a spark in his eyes Jabbar had never seen before.

He knew Mushtaq had a point. Let Iqbal and his men do some drama for the time being. They would join him eventually as they had no other option left.

He was soft with Iqbal and his crew. He would get tough if they wouldn't agree to join him. He was determined to kill anyone who refused to join him.

***

Mushtaq rushed out to convey the message to Iqbal. "You can start shooting Iqbal." He took out bidi and offered one to Iqbal. Both lit bidis and smoked.

Iqbal smiled at Shweta. She smiled back. The dimples on her cheeks deepened when she smiled. She looked prettier. She touched Iqbal's hand as if to extend her warm support. She silently appreciated his magical move. In the middle of the deadly terrorists who were threatening to kill them, Iqbal convinced them for film shooting. Unbelievable!

Iqbal instructed Shweta, "We have to get going." Shweta took the bidi from Iqbal's hand and sucked on it. She hated when Iqbal smoked or boozed alone.

"Without Prabhas?" Shweta handed the bidi back to him.

"We will shoot the portion where he is not required. We will do the song today." Iqbal came up with a solution, "Where is Crystal?"

"She is in the vanity van." Shweta said.

Iqbal headed to the vanity van with Shweta, Mallika, Mastani and Chandni. "Call everyone near the vanity van." Iqbal whispered.

Almost everyone gathered close to the vanity van. Crystal came out of the vanity van and sat on the steps. Abbas came and asked them, "What is happening here?" He was unhappy.

"Bhai has asked me to start shooting," Iqbal replied, "We are getting ready for that."

Abbas looked at Bilal. Bilal had a long & deep scar in the middle of his forehead, a knife mark which made him look deadly. He was stout with a bald head, long-beard and a cruel face. Just the sight of Abbas or Bilal was enough to scare anyone. Their faces were brutal and eyes full of hatred. Both rushed to talk to Mushtaq.

Iqbal spoke in a low voice when they left, "Good news is we can start the filming right now. This is a golden opportunity for us."

"How can we shoot under the surveillance of these hard-core terrorists?" Crystal was apprehensive.

"Have you all seen James Bond films?" Iqbal surprised everyone with that question. It was out of context, but he continued talking, "Why audience likes James Bond movies? They know its fiction and its predictable. The hero would be victorious at the end. They watch it for the adventure. Life without adventure is boring." Iqbal looked at everyone, "God has given us a golden opportunity for that kind of adventure in real life. We have been abducted. We are living 24x7 with dreaded terrorists and yet, shooting our film -*Azadi*." He sighed and continued, "Imagine tomorrow, years later, your kids will be telling this story to your grandchildren. Would they believe you? No. It is an unbelievable situation. It's unique." Iqbal paused and said, "This is chance to make friends." Iqbal looked at it as a golden opportunity to get the terrorists involved.

Iqbal motivated everyone. He saw a spark in their eyes and a smile on their lips.

***

Abbas talked to Mushtaq. "I want to meet Bhai."

No one could go in the den without Mushtaq's permission, "What is it?"

"These people preparing for shooting here." Abbas was angry.

"Yes, they are. Bhai has given permission."

"Hmm." Abbas looked at him. He knew Bhai's decision was final. He would be killed if he questioned his decision. *But, how could he?* He wasn't happy at all.

***

The film unit was ready to experience the adventure.

The crew wanted to mingle with the terrorists and make friends during the shooting of the film.

Mushtaq, Omar, Salim and Tipu found a few boxes when they went inside the black SUV. They took out whisky, rum, beer & vodka bottles. Mushtaq shared with everyone. Guddu and Rafee served them some dry fruits.

Iqbal asked the choreographers Mastani and Mallika to organize and rehearse the song. Chandni smiled looking at Mushtaq. Chandni was carrying a huge bag full of costumes.

"Hello!" Chandni initiated. Mushtaq blushed. Omar smiled at Mushtaq. He knew Mushtaq was interested in talking to her. Mushtaq looked at the bags she was carrying.

"What's in the bags?" Asked Mushtaq

"Costumes."

"What exactly do you do?" Mushtaq started a conversation with Chandni. He was a little tipsy. Chandni realised that. Mushtaq offered to help carry the bags.

"I am a costume designer." Chandni said which he hardly understood. She knew he didn't, "The work is divided into different departments to run things smoothly. Everyone is responsible for something or the other. I look after the costumes of the artists. What dress will suit the situation and the artist- I decide." She explained it.

Chandni went inside the vanity van. Mushtaq followed her in.

Mushtaq was shocked to see the interiors of the vanity van.

It had mirrors, couch and bed etc. Chandni went out with a few dresses leaving Mushtaq inside the van alone.

He called Tipu, Salim, Omar, Afzal, Karim and Changez to see the van. They were all surprised to see a van that was more like a tiny posh house from inside.

"Wow! Amazing!" Salim plonked himself on the soft couch.

Mastani and Mallika entered the van with a few dancers. They saw the terrorists inside and stepped out. Chandni reassured them and called them in again. Chandni had made friends with Mushtaq already. Often they gazed at each other. They seldom spoke but exchanged looks and it was leading to a silent mutual attraction.

Mushtaq smiled at her. Chandni smiled back and hinted with

little finger that she wanted to pee. Mushtaq didn't understand why she was telling him that? *She wanted to go to the loo. She could go. Did she want him to accompany her?* He was confused.

"Do you want me to come with you?" Mushtaq offered help.

"I want you and your friends to go out. We need to use the washroom." Chandni chuckled and said in a friendly way.

Mushtaq smiled and left with all his friends.

"It has a washroom too!" he said to hide his embarrassment.

"Yes. What did you think? If it has a couch, a bed and mirrors, why not a washroom? It is simple," Omar tried to show off his knowledge, "A full apartment inside a van!"

Muhstaq felt like an idiot for a moment. Why couldn't he guess that? It was easy- common sense. He took out his bidi and lit it.

***

Shabbir Mallik and Muneer Lone had their breakfast.

Muneer Lone looked at his fingers. His nails were over grown. They needed clipping.

Muneer broke the silence, "If Jabbar sends a corpse, army will take action for sure."

"Yes, they will." Shabbir tried to understand where he was going with this question.

"If army conducts an operation, Jabbar and his men might get killed." Lone continued, "This government is on the hot seat, ready to attack anyone and everyone without a delay."

"Possible." Shabbir responded coolly.

"Don't you think, Jabbar is thinking the same way?" He said as if he solved a puzzle, "That's why Jabbar didn't send the body."

Muneer raised a valid point.

Shabbir countered him, "Jabbar doesn't think, I think for Jabbar Ellahi."

Shabbir said confidently, his voice was loud and clear, "I made him Jabbar Ellahi. He was Amir Hussain. He used to pelt stones at the army on the streets." Shabbir Mallik explained, "No one is Jabbar Ellahi. Jabbar Ellahi is a brand we make, which will never die. Many Amirs will come and go, but Jabbar Ellahi will live forever."

Muneer Lone understood his frustration.

They were waiting for the big bang. Shabbir trusted Jabbar. They hoped the bodies would create a havoc and bring the government on its knees. Shabbir was under pressure from people who invested in him. Big money, trust and prestige were at stake.

Both were worried about the situation.

The plan was executed successfully, then what went wrong? Why Jabbar didn't fulfill his commitment?

"Okay, I will leak it to my friends in the media." Lone spoke after a long thought, "Let the news spread and government know that it wasn't an accident, but kidnapping."

Shabbir Mallik smiled. That it was a good idea.

***

The news of movie crew abduction spread like wildfire.

Entire Bollywood was shocked. It became the nation's biggest gossip. Channels were overflowing with debates on the future of the '*Azadi*' crew along with Kashmir and Pakistan issues.

The television race began for a new TRP story.

Prabhas Venkatesh made a statement in a press conference, "It is a difficult time for the hostages and their families."

"How did you escape?" One of the reporters asked.

"I didn't escape. I was saved. God wanted me to come back safe."

"God wanted the rest of the crew members unsafe?" A reporter asked him. He had no reply.

Prabhas was upset. Media asked stupid questions to humiliate him. He had worked hard to reach this position. Today he was rich and famous. But he always had a problem with journalists. He hated them. He had a few friends in media but most of them were uncontrollable.

***

"How did the abduction news leak?" Ajit Dayal lost his cool with Rudra Shekhar.

"I think one of the separatist leaders leaked it." Shekhar replied, "It was viral on the internet first. A London based wire did it, the news came from Syria, Dubai, Malaysia and London. No one is vouching for its authenticity."

"Separatist leaders?" Ajit doubted.

"I think so," Shekhar speculated, "The terrorists could do it."

"Hmm." Dayal was wrapping his head around the idea.

CHAPTER 11

New Delhi 7, Race Course Road.

The PM sipped his tea and looked at the home minister Amit Singh Thakur.

"Someone leaked it. It claims that the movie crew is held hostage by the terrorists. Media reported it. We must clarify it in a press conference."

"Who is this someone? It must be separatist leaders abroad."

"Yes, I agree with you on that!"

Both were contemplative.

"Do you think they have taken them to the other side of the fence?" PM expressed his concern.

No one replied. No one knew anything about it. They suspected it. They couldn't deny the possibility of it. If indeed the hostages were taken across the border, it could lead to an explosive situation.

Ajit Dayal didn't touch his tea. He was busy reading and sending messages to his people in Pakistan and Afghanistan and was trying to gather information from his sources.

"This was well planned." Ajit broke the silence, "Separatist leaders all over the globe have supported it."

They discussed this grave issue which drew their attention. Everyone agreed that nothing warranted action now. They had to wait for some action from the terrorists and then retaliate.

They continued the discussion and put people on the job.

CHAPTER 12

The filming began under the vigilance of hard-core terrorists on the hill plateau. Everyone was convinced that Iqbal was right; they would be killed if they were scared. Most of the terrorists were drunk and relaxed after a long time. They were thanking Mushtaq.

"I found it. They were not sharing it with us. I found it from the SUV. These bastards keep bottles and drink while they travel." Mushtaq flaunted the brandy bottles in his hand.

They felt jealous of the life the crew had.

"Only Iqbal could do this." Shweta smiled and said to Crystal.

Crystal met Iqbal for the first time when they were shooting on the hills of Panchgani. It was an action movie *Lock In*. She had little else to do except to run behind the hero. Iqbal was the first AD. He was very active, and he worked almost as a ghost director.

He used to fix cameras, lenses, lights, and narrate the scene to her.

A few months later he approached her with a new script. It was an amazing love story titled *Azadi*. She took no time to say yes to Iqbal.

"Have you got the investor?" She asked.

"Looking for one!" Iqbal said. He didn't turn up for a while.

Crystal knew Iqbal would take some time. She was happy for Iqbal and supported him. She even took a cut in her pay and agreed to come to Kashmir for the shoot when the same script came through Lalawani's manager.

Iqbal was courageous. He faced Jabbar Ellahi fearlessly. Crystal was totally impressed with him when he said he would like to be the first to die. *How the hell did he convince such a dreaded terrorist for a movie shoot?* He had a right positive attitude. "Make friends with them and they wouldn't kill." He was so right! He was ready to shoot his film without the protagonist.

Shweta was standing with him shoulder to shoulder. Not just her, every crew member supported Iqbal in every possible way.

***

The shoot began with a dance number. Mastani and Mallika were ready with their beautiful dancers. Crystal was dancing in the center. The song had a quick beat. Iqbal was taking shots. A part of the song was played over and over again by the recordist Prashant Mukherjee. Iqbal was busy taking best of shots. He was running from pillar to post. He was asking KK to move the camera, watching dancers, making Mallika and Mastani understand the kind of sequences he wanted. Shweta was attentive and helped him do his best.

Mushtaq was watching everything with a lot of interest but his focus was at Chandni.

The terrorists had never experienced anything akin to a film shoot. They were having a ball of a time. They relished the delicious food three times a day and gazed at glamourous girls dancing with booze in their hands.

The treacherous hilltop plateau was turned in to an outdoor location for shooting for the moment. Mushtaq climbed up on top of the bus to watch the shooting better. Chandni's eyes were searching for Mushtaq. She heard a whistle and spotted him. He waved his hand to her and she smiled. He was thrilled. He invited her up with a stylish flick of a hand.

Chandni tried climbing on top of the bus taking support of the thin stirs at the back of the bus. She was scrambling. Mushtaq saw her struggle.

"Can you give me a hand?" Chandni requested.

"Yes. Sure." Mushtaq extended his hand to her.

Mushtaq felt a 440 volts current going through him when he touched Chandni. Chandni came up and stood right next to him. She saw the trench. She was about to lose her balance. Mushtaq held her. She let him hold her. They were very close to each other for a few moments. Chandni got conscious and shifted away.

"Thank you." Chandni said while looking around, "I was about to fall."

"I would never let you fall." Mushtaq didn't believe he just said that. It happened so fast. He really liked her. Chandni saw few beer bottles kept there.

"What is this?" She asked.

"Do you want one?"

"I don't mind."

Both had a beer and looked around. Abbas and Bilal watched him jealously.

Chandni saw the view- the greenery, the trench and the waterfall.

"Awesome." Chandni couldn't take her eyes off the splendor around, "It is amazing!" Mushtaq gazed at Chandni longingly, who was mesmerized with the view.

Why on earth was he happy when she was feeling happy? He didn't get an answer.

Salim and Omar were watching him too.

"Who is that?" Chandni noticed the men on the platforms made on treetops. "They are guarding us. Anyone trying to enter would be shot immediately. Mansoor, Akbar, Murid, Kazi..." Mushtaq introduced them all, "They are sharpshooters." Mushtaq didn't mention that they would shoot any of the film crew, if they tried to escape.

Why did he not mention that? Mushtaq found a change in himself. He didn't say it because he was softening.

Mastani walked on one side and sat on a rock. She caught Omar staring at her. Omar looked like a typical Kashmiri youth. Underaged young boy with fair skin and a broad forehead. Omar liked Mastani - sexy, whitish, tall and very graceful.

Mastani started the conversation, "How do you like all this?" She invited him to sit next to her on the same rock with a nod.

"Fine." Omar said while sitting down. He sweated as she moved closer. It was unexpected. He could barely talk.

"You want to suggest any dance movements?"

"Good. This is good." Omar wanted to talk a lot but he was shy by nature. Salim noticed Omar and Mastani mingling.

***

Jabbar came out of his den to pee.

He looked for Tipu, Salim, Omar and Mushtaq. He found none.

Iqbal was busy filming. Jabbar's men were busy watching the shooting. They didn't care where their guns were!

Jabbar peed in a corner in an open space and came back to them and tried to announce his presence. He coughed to draw attention. But no one noticed. Where was Mushtaq? He wasn't around. He looked up and saw him with Chandni. Jabbar was shocked to see him flirting with Chandni.

Have they gone mad or what? Have they never seen girls in their lives? He coughed again. This time loudly. Salim and Omar noticed him. Omar came to him immediately. Salim followed.

"What is going on here?" Jabbar looked upset and angry, "Has he become a monkey!" He pointed at Mushtaq.

Salim and Omar made noises so that Mushtaq could hear them. Mushtaq was too busy talking to Chandni. He heard nothing at all.

"Honestly speaking, looking at you, no one can say that you would kill people." Chandni praised Mushtaq, "To me you are very kind and friendly. Girls like men like you."

"Really? You think so?" Mushtaq pretended to be oblivious but felt great.

Jabbar ignored Mushtaq. He moved around and started scolding his men who were busy watching girls and shooting, leaving their guns aside.

***

Iqbal was busy taking shots when he heard noises. He got distracted.

"Silence please." Iqbal said politely. The noises didn't stop.

"Silence!" He said again. The noises still didn't stop.

"Who is this? How many times have I said 'Silence!" Iqbal was loud this time. Before he could understand anything, he was slapped. It was none other than Tipu. Jabbar was standing right behind him.

"How dare you silence Bhai." Tipu roared.

"Sorry I was engrossed in my work."

"Work?" Jabber mocked, "You call this work?"

Iqbal was quiet. Shweta and Crystal hung their heads.

Mushtaq finally took notice. He jumped down from the bus.

Mushtaq stood in front of Jabbar looking guilty.

"Where were you?" Jabbar asked.

"Close by. Observing everything from the top, so that..." Mushtaq pretended as though he was working and not flirting with a girl.

"So that?" Jabbar wanted him to complete the sentence. He got the smell and knew he was drinking.

"Everything should work as per our plan." Mushtaq added smartly.

Jabbar headed for his den. He was serious.

He knew Shabbir would call again.

He was continuously thinking of an apt reply to give Shabbir.

***

"Have you forgotten your purpose?" Jabbar looked at Omar, Tipu, Salim, Mushtaq, "We take shelter in these dense hills for this? Our lives have been dedicated to Kashmir. Do you remember? Or have you forgotten?"

"Yes Bhai. Kashmir's freedom is our purpose."

"We live hardest of lives, we sleep on floors, walk through knee-deep snow, even when we are unwell. Right...?"

"Right Bhai."

"We should always remember that. Never ever forget that nothing happens without a sacrifice." Jabbar sensed the silence. "What are you guys waiting for? Call the filmi honcho and record the statement." Jabbar shouted.

Everyone left to call Iqbal.

***

Iqbal was summoned in the den.

He stood like a schoolboy who had done something wrong and was about to be punished. "You have forgotten so soon." Jabbar was angry, "We have to send the message to the Indian government."

"I was waiting for your orders Bhai," Iqbal said smartly, "We will send it right now."

KK set up the camera with a monitor.

Jabbar was ready to deliver his message to Indian government.

We need a strong, very strong message to shake the entire nation. Jabbar thought and was excited to speak.

"Have you thought about your speech?" Iqbal asked politely.

"What speech?"

"I mean our message to the Indian government." Iqbal explained the purpose, "This video will be seen worldwide."

"If you think the government will leak that video - you are an idiot," Jabbar, Mushtaq, Salim and Omar laughed at Iqbal.

Iqbal listened to them quietly and made his point, "We will, if they won't. We will send it to different mobiles phones on all social media- WhatsApp groups, Facebook, Instagram, all internet platforms. That video will go viral. Everyone is interested in the movie crew you abducted."

"There is no network here." Omar said.

"Fine. You must be having friends in the media; they would do it. It will spread like wild fire." Iqbal showed the way.

"We have friends all the over world. Pakistan, Syria, Dubai, London everywhere. That is not the issue, but Bhai can't show his face." Mushtaq pointed out another problem.

"Put on a mask." Iqbal was quick.

"We don't have masks." Omar said.

"We will make one." Iqbal looked at Shweta and asked her to make one out of black cloth they used for the camera.

Jabbar thought for a while and came up with a few lines.

"Insha'Allah, this land will be flooded with blood and flesh of the movie crew. I will blow their heads from their shoulders with bombs. I will kill everyone. Reinstate Article 370 or I will massacre them all in one go. Do it in twenty-four hours or I will kill all." he paused, raised his hand and said, "Freedom! Freedom!"

Jabbar looked at Iqbal for appreciation.

Iqbal was quiet. He didn't want to say anything negative, "This is good but..." He stopped for a while. Mushtaq gazed at him, he didn't like the pause Iqbal took.

"You did well." Mushtaq encouraged him, "What say you Iqbal?"

"I want something even more powerful." Iqbal said in a low voice.

"Why don't you try something. Bhai might like it." Mushtaq suggested. Iqbal liked the idea; he chewed his nails for a moment and took the pen and wrote something down.

He read out the lines for Jabbar, "You can suck out all our blood, chop our bodies, cut our flesh in to pieces, do whatever you want to do with us but, we wouldn't allow you to take an inch of Kashmir. We would fight till the end of our last breath for Kashmir. For the freedom of Kashmir! Insha'Allah, we will take Kashmir from you." Iqbal looked at Jabbar, "You know what is justice? A real justice is Allah's justice. You removed Article 370 from the constitution to enslave us. Allah has sent 370 Indians to us. We will kill all 370 Indians if article 370 is not reinstated." Iqbal stunned everyone. He read it with proper voice modulations, intonations and pauses.

Jabbar loved it. He smiled. He wanted to pat Iqbal's back, but he stopped himself. Iqbal spoke like he was one of them.

"Practice it please. Shweta, help him say the lines." Iqbal spoke like a film director helping his artist read the dialogues.

Shweta read the lines for Jabbar. He practiced the lines without the mask on. KK had kept the camera on and filmed Jabbar.

Jabbar was ready with the lines.

"Should we go for it, Sir?" Iqbal asked politely.

"Yes, we can." Jabbar was confident. Jabbar Ellahi delivered the monologue twice and the rest watched the monitor.

Jabbar stood alone after he finished his dialogue. He didn't know what to do as everyone was busy watching him on the monitor. So, Jabbar walked slowly and stood behind them. Everyone was bent or knelt down to watch the monitor on the floor.

"Re-wind it a bit." Iqbal asked Aman. He re-wound and cued it.

Iqbal wanted to watch the footage of Jabbar rehearsing the lines without his mask.

"Awesome! Camera just loves him. He is very photogenic." KK looked at Jabbar's appearance and said. Iqbal kept looking at Jabbar's footage. "He looks like a Hollywood star." He looked at Shweta. She agreed with Iqbal, "Yes he is. He has got charisma and a great screen presence," Shweta admitted.

Aman, Mushtaq, Salim and Omar's eyes were glued to the monitor. All admired his appearance.

Jabbar enjoyed watching himself on the screen standing silently behind. He went with the flow and enjoyed their admiration.

Iqbal stood up and looked at him, "We are all proud of you." Jabbar blushed with Mushtaq's compliments. "You look handsome Bhai."

"Ammi use to say I look like a hero." Jabbar didn't realize when he blurted it out. It just came out spontaneously. He was stunned for a moment. Something stung him. He found everyone staring at him. *Oh God! What did I say?* He was embarrassed so he got worked up and irritated. He kicked the monitor and slapped Aman who was standing close to him.

"Get out! Get lost!" He shouted.

Everyone left the den immediately.

CHAPTER 13

The threatening video was sent on a pen drive and immediately delivered to Shabbir.

Shabbir Mallik and Muneer Lone watched the video over and over again. Shabbir uploaded it and emailed it to his digital media team sitting in London, Dubai, and Syria.

"They were happy to see it. He would kill all 370 people in one go. Jabbar is very intelligent. He is negotiating with the government to reinstate 370 or he would kill all. Great! He is my kid. I am proud of him." Shabbir cheered loudly.

Muneer Lone heard him patiently and asked, "That was his plan. He didn't have dysentery." Lone warned him to be careful of his soldier. He was using his mind. He was thinking.

Shabbir agreed, albeit hesitantly. Jabbar had taken this decision on his own. Was he slipping from Shabbir's clutches? No he wasn't. Had that been the case, he would not send the video.

Jabbar always obeyed his orders. This time too he would follow his instructions. Nothing to worry, everything was under his control.

***

Jabbar Ellahi's video went viral globally.

"370 Versus 370" was the headline of the leading national news channel - India Today. The afternoon tabloid of Lutyens Delhi copied India Today's headline as it was perfectly written by the chief editor Rajdeep. Soon it was available on the internet and social media platforms. Almost every smart mobile phone had Jabbar's threatening video.

Iqbal and Jabbar were discussed across the globe.

Before Bollywood made any statement, all Hollywood stars made an appeal to Jabbar not to kill innocent creative people.

The bookies started betting on hostage's life- 'Will they be alive or be killed by the terrorists.'

Pakistani media called it freedom fighter's victory. Though the prime minister of Pakistan Imran Khan appealed to Jabbar and his friends 'Not to kill innocent people.' Later he changed his statement after the Pakistani army chief Qamar Javed Bajwa cautioned him. Imran then avoided any appealing and focused on the issue of freedom for Kashmir.

For Pakistan, their own economic crisis was not important. Kashmir was more important. The celebrations began in Pakistan. Videos were made and sent out on social media to irk Indians.

***

The PM, home minister, defense minister and the entire cabinet were worried. What would happen if he killed them? They left to talk to their teams to find out some solution, leaving the PM alone. He sighed deeply.

The PM saw the video time and again. These people didn't learn lessons easily.

***

Sampit Jena was ready to address the media. He was waiting for everyone to calm down as the conference hall was noisy and overcrowded. He spoke after a while.

"We have a difficult situation here. Members of our film fraternity have been abducted in large numbers by Jabbar Ellahi, an ill-famed terrorist. He has demanded article 370 to be reinstated in the state of J&K. The government has appealed to free all 370-innocent people immediately and then the government will discuss the possibilities. Killing innocent people wouldn't solve any problems," He paused, "Anything is possible in a peaceful situation. Violence has no place."

The reporters were ready to shoot questions. Which he refused to reply at that moment. "I will soon be in a position to take your questions. I have to attend a meeting with the senior ministers." Sampit said and left.

***

Bollywood Federation's (the mother body of all film associations) president B. N. Tiwari released an appeal to the terrorists.

An appeal letter duly signed by all top film producers, directors and artists was sent to PM and later, posted on social media platforms in anticipation that it would go viral and finally reach Jabbbar Ellahi.

Prabhas Venkatesh met the Prime Minister and posted his photos with PM to prove that he was trying his best to rescue the hijacked film crew.

The American President warned the terrorists of dire consequences if they killed innocent creative artists.

CHAPTER 14

Jabbar Ellahi got a call on his satellite phone from Shabbir Mallik.

"It is a wise decision to kill them all in one go." Shabbir appreciated his stand, "I am proud of you. When do you want to do it?" asked Mallik.

"I think, I should wait for their reply." Jabbar replied. He was not asking but taking decisions on his own, "If they are willing to comply with our demand then we work on our next plan."

And what was their next plan? Jabbar didn't discuss with him.

Shabbir hung up and decided to wait and watch.

Jabbar didn't want to discuss anything with Shabbir. He was his own master, making decisions without consulting him. But why? What went wrong? Things were okay till Jabbar executed his plan.

Mushtaq listened to Jabbar's conversation with Shabbir.

Mushtaq happily headed out to see what Iqbal and his crew planned to shoot next. He was curious about Chandni.

CHAPTER 15

Chandni was chatting with Mastani and Mallika.

"Have they finished all the bottles they got?" Mallika asked.

"I think so." Chandni replied. She glanced at Mushtaq, Tipu, Omar and Salim who were sitting at a distance.

"I know what is going on between you and this chic." Tipu said when Mushtaq smiled at Chandni. She smiled back. Tipu noticed it. He gave Mushtaq a knowing smile.

"Are you mad?" Mushtaq blushed, "Do you think she is interested in me?" Mushtaq wanted to confirm.

"She would never had gone on top of that bus if she was not interested." Tipu had drawn his own conclusion. Mushtaq was happy, "I don't know what Allah's wish is!" He chuckled and said, "He sent her for me."

"Can you do me a favor?" Tipu looked at Mushtaq.

"Can you talk to Chandni if she can..." Tipu reluctant to say anything further.

"She what...?" Mushtaq was curious.

"If she can talk to Mallika." Tipu felt shy and whispered, "I just want to be friends, that's it."

"That's it? Only friendship?" Mushtaq confirmed.

"Yes. Only that."

"I will talk to her. Don't worry. Make sure that Bhai doesn't know about it."

"He will know one day." Tipu said just like that.

"Make sure he doesn't know, if you and I want to live." Mushtaq warned him. Mushtaq was worried that news of his blossoming romance will reach Jabbar.

"You need to be smart. That's it. If you are not alert, you would meet with an accident and die. So better be alert." He made him understand. "Lie smartly and live smartly. That is the rule of the game."

Tipu had never seen Mushtaq like this before. He was meeting a new Muhstaq.

Mushtaq washed his face and headed to the rock where Mastani, Mallika and Chandni were sitting.

"Hello!" Mushtaq smiled at the three of them.

"Hi Mushtaq!" Chandni smiled back.

"Can you come here for a minute?" Mushtaq requested Chandni. She got up immediately and came close to Mushtaq.

"Tipu wants to make friends with Mallika." Mushtaq whispered. Chandni smiled and asked naughtily, "What am I getting in return?" She smiled looking at Mushtaq, "It will be done in no time but I want a gift."

"What do you want?" Mushtaq continued flirting.

"Hmm, that will be due on you." Chandni smartly took his promise. She called Mallika and introduced her to Tipu.

"Why are you not shooting?" Tipu asked Mallika when they were formally introduced. They walked to the corner. Chandni and Mushtaq walked with them. Mallika followed behind them.

"Only Iqbal can answer your question." Mallika smiled.

"Why don't you ask him?" Chandni instigated him, she wanted everyone to be engaged in filming.

***

Iqbal sipped tea Guddu served and asked him, "Are you scared?"

"No. I was, but not now." Guddu was young, just 21. He was quick and energetic. He always looked for a chance to talk to Iqbal.

Shweta and Crystal came and picked up mugs of tea and sat quietly.

"Everyone must have got the video we shot." Shweta said.

"Hmm." Iqbal agreed. Both knew Iqbal was contemplating ways to get out of their sticky situation.

"Has everyone had their breakfast?" Iqbal asked Kabir.

"Yes." Kabir replied and joined them. Mushtaq, Mallika, Chandni, Mastani, Salim and Omar walked towards them.

Mushtaq came and asked, "What happened? Why you are not shooting?"

Iqbal stood up walked with him, keeping his hand on Mushtaq's shoulder as if they both have been friends for years.

Shweta, Crystal and Kabir looked at Mushtaq and Iqbal as they were leaving. Crystal smiled.

"I have a request, a humble request…" Mushtaq stopped suddenly when Iqbal said that. He knew by now that Iqbal was street smart. He had some plans which might put him in trouble. Mushtaq was alert, "Tell me straight, don't twist the matter man, come to the point." Iqbal looked at him.

Omar, Salim and Tipu knew Mushtaq was deadly and smarter than Iqbal. Being a man Friday to Jabbar Bhai was not a joke.

Mushtaq took all the calls for Jabbar Ellahi and he honored it.

"You are very powerful and might have contacts all over."

"What is the matter with you Iqbal? Tell me, come on, what do you want?" Mushtaq was irritated.

"Kidnap Prabhas Venkatesh!"

"You mean the movie star Prabhas Venkatesh?"

"Yes. He is the hero of my film. The day you abducted us, he was unwell and stayed back at his room in Hotel India Pride Srinagar. We need him to continue the shooting brother."

"Not possible." Mushtaq reacted sharply, "The army has cordoned off the area. Police and army on every inch of the soil. And Prabhas Venkatesh would have left by now. He is not a hero he portrays on the silver screen- he is a coward. I bet he took the first flight available and left Srinagar." Mushtaq mocked.

"He owns a private jet. He is very rich." Iqbal agreed with him, "He would have gone by now."

Both looked at each other.

"What now? Take someone else from your unit and make him a hero. Start the shooting."

"It's not that simple. You can't make anyone and everyone a hero. To become a hero of a film is a big thing. People spend their time and money and sit in cinema halls to watch the film despite having many other options. They can watch the movie later on different media – TV, internet, mobile & digital platforms. They can watch it free on Netflix or Amazon – but they choose to go to the theatres," He paused, "Because they see their hero on big silver screen – larger than life image in every possible way. You can't just pick any Tom, Dick or Harry and make him a hero." Iqbal looked at Mushtaq to gauge his level of comprehension.

Three of them watched Iqbal with their mouths wide open.

"Oh really! It's a tough decision to make." Mushtaq joked as he thought Iqbal was making a mountain out of a molehill, "So according to you there is no one here who can be a hero of a film and replace Prabhas Venkatesh?"

Iqbal was silent. He looked around. He didn't reply. Mushtaq was looking at him for an answer. He knew Iqbal would come up with something unpredictable. He tried to read his mind.

"None, except one."

"Except one? Who is the lucky one?" Omar made fun of Iqbal.

But Mushtaq was serious. He wanted to hear the name while Tipu, Salim and Omar were laughing.

Iqbal let the three of them laugh. He knew Mushtaq had some idea who he was talking about. And he was so right.

"Are you…" Mushtaq couldn't complete. Salim and Omar caught on and were suddenly serious.

"Yes! Bhai, Jabbar Bhai. He can be the hero of my movie. He can replace Prabhas – no one else." Iqbal said it with conviction. Mushtaq, Salim, Omar and Tipu exchanged looks. They insinuated Tipu to convey the message to Jabbar Ellahi. He understood their hint.

"No, no, no. I am not going." Mushtaq looked at him with stern eyes to make him obey his orders. He had no option.

Eventually Tipu went in the den. Three of them heard Jabbar Ellahi's loud angry shouting. Tipu was back with his clothes torn. He had been beaten.

"See, I told you. He would have killed me." He complained.

"Go and change, you are almost naked." Salim drew his attention to the girls. He left immediately. Crystal and Shweta were trying to understand what happened.

They came and stood beside Mushtaq and Iqbal. Iqbal smiled looking at them. Mushtaq and Salim smiled too.

"What happened to Tipu?"

"Nothing. We are trying to sort something out." Iqbal pacified everybody.

"Let's go inside and talk to Bhai." Iqbal proposed something unexpected.

"Have you gone mad. Haven't you seen how badly Tipu was beaten up just now."

"I will convince him. What will happen at the end of the day? He will beat me up. I am ready to be beaten for *Azadi*."

"*Azadi*?" Mushtaq repeated immediately.

"My film. Name of my movie- *Azadi*." Iqbal clarified.

"Oh that! I am not doing that talking. I will be standing."

"Don't worry Mushtaq Bhai."

***

Jabbar turned his neck slowly to look at Iqbal. Mushtaq was hiding behind Iqbal. *How dare he suggest it? Me and a filmi hero? Has he gone nuts? What does he think of himself? I cannot be taken for granted. Iqbal crossed his limits. Tipu came with this proposal and got beaten badly. Despite that, he comes with this idiotic proposal. How dare he!* Jabbar's mind was a chatterbox. Jabbar was about to kick him out of the den. Then he saw Crystal.

She walked down and stood at the entrance of the den. She heard about the proposal. She wanted to talk to Iqbal about it. She stayed and waited for Iqbal to finish his business with Jabbar and then she would discuss it with him.

"How dare you. Do I look like a joker?" Jabbar broke the silence.

"Hero Bhai! You look like a hero." Iqbal continued without any hesitation, "I just want to make one last point if I may…"

Jabbar scoffed as if he was tired of Iqbal's justification.

"Leave it." Mushtaq knew Jabbar Bhai would never agree to it.

"It's a smart move. Trust me. See, no one lives forever. Death will come sooner or later. But through this movie you can live forever. Let the world know who Jabbar was. A freedom fighter or…" he took a pause and continued, "This film will release worldwide. The whole world will know, he is the same Jabbar Ellahi who dodged the government of India and became the hero of '*Azadi*'. Think about it! No one can ever imagine that. You will make a monkey out of the government of India." Iqbal paused for effect, "A Film never dies. This movie would go in the theatres, after that on television sets in every household, mobile phone, internet and all future formats. People will see you, love you… you will live forever." Iqbal added, "It is chance to show the world who Jabbar Ellahi is."

He stopped for response after extempore impressive speech.

Iqbal made everyone think about it. Silence prevailed. Everyone was introspecting. In the meantime, Crystal called Iqbal.

"Can I have a word with you?" Iqbal moved to her.

She whispered when Iqbal stood close to her, "What are you doing? Have you consulted me before you offered that role to him? I was cast against Prabhas. He wouldn't be able to do it. He is a good-looking guy, that is fine but believe me he can't perform. Why are you spoiling your film? Don't go for it. He can't do it." She said and left the den.

Jabbar noticed the beautiful lady for the first time. He was least interested in women and hardly noticed them. But he noticed her. She had long hair, fair skin, cute smile, dimples on her cheek, full breasts – she was like a Kashmiri girl. Jabbar didn't like her whispering. What did she tell Iqbal? All he could understand that the conversation was about him.

"What did she just say?" Jabbar asked.

"Ignore her. She can't understand your caliber as an actor. I know."

"But what did she say? I want to know." Jabbar insisted.

"She was apprehensive about your performance." Iqbal spoke in low voice.

"Is she saying I can't do that shit work you guys do?" Jabbar was worked up.

Mushtaq found the right time to interject, "She doesn't know anything. Bhai's appearance would ignite the silver screen."

"He would create magic," Iqbal added the fuel, "He has that kind of charisma which will make the audience go crazy. But…"

"What is this but – do you also think like her." Mushtaq asked.

"No. I have full confidence in Bhai. Bhai should teach her a lesson by doing just one scene. What do you think Mushtaq?"

"Surely it's nothing for Bhai. He has done real life action, killed many, just like that and blew buses by pressing a trigger. What is this…? Nothing at all."

"It's nothing. Just reading some lines in front of the camera. Just like we made that video. That's it!" Iqbal made it sound easy.

***

Jabbar was ready to perform. He stood in front of the camera. Shweta was rehearsing the lines with Jabbar. The dress man Kishore, brought the jeans and T-shirt for Jabbar Ellahi.

"He is from London, he wears western clothes." Iqbal requested.

"Who is he?" frowned Jabbar.

"Azad. The protagonist," Iqbal clarified, "Azad is our hero fighting for Azadi."

"Hmm." Jabbar looked at Mushtaq. He walked with Jabbar to his den to change. Salim, Omar, Abbas, Bilal, Changez, Kadar, Abrar and the entire unit watched him.

Iqbal entered the den and suggested Jabbar's beard needed to be shaved, he did that too.

Jabbar Ellahi walked out clean shaven, in jeans and T shirt.

He looked like a star.

"Wow!" Jabbar heard Crystal's voice. He didn't know how to respond to that. Navin (make up man) came forward for his makeup.

He recalled what he had said the previous night when he was supposed to kill Iqbal. He slapped Navin.

Navin fell at a distance. Iqbal intervened.

"Didn't I tell you I hate it." Jabbar said and looked at Iqbal, "I am a man, not a woman."

"It's not makeup Bhai, it is touch up. Just below your eyes, to conceal your dark circles." Iqbal was polite when she said that, "These dark circles are making you look ..." Iqbal didn't complete the sentence.

"Look what...?" Asked Jabbar

"You are looking absolutely great but below your eyes these dark circles..."

Mushtaq came forward, "I will shoot you Iqbal. Complete the sentence. Do you want to say that it's not make-up just touch up for the dark circles, not for the entire face?" He tried to solve the issue.

"I meant exactly that."

Mushtaq smiled, "Bhai has no issue with that I think."

Iqbal signaled Navin. Navin did a slight make up. Jabbar sat quietly through the process.

Mallika noticed Abbas eyeing her. He looked at her cleavage and smiled cunningly. Mallika didn't like it. She got up, headed to Mastani who was standing close to Omar and Tipu. Abbas kept staring at her.

Jabbar was busy rehearsing the lines. Shweta was explaining the lines to him. "*I can stop the storm & melt the mountain. I will bring the sky on to your toes and kick the entire earth like a football,*" She paused, "You have to hug her and continue – *I can do anything for you sweetheart. I love you.*" Jabbar practiced the lines.

He was ready for the take. Everyone watched expectantly.

The camera was rolled. Iqbal said 'Action'.

"I can …" Jabbar forgot the line. Crystal hugged him. Her touch was magical. He was thrilled, goosebumps all over him. Her soft skin and flesh mesmerized him. Her fragrance intoxicated him. He had never come so close to a woman before, except his mother. Crystal's big breasts, beautiful smile, magical touch and expressive eyes made him forget his lines completely. He was nervous.

Fifty takes went waste with no positive results. Crystal was tired of hugging Jabbar. Arjun, the last assistant with clap was exhausted banging claps fifty times.

Jabbar was disappointed in himself. He could do it, he knew. But performing in front of the camera was proving to be far more difficult than he imagined.

By now all the terrorists had the lines by heart and they started practicing the lines to understand what was so difficult. They practiced. While they practiced, they imagined hugging Crystal. They lifted their hands in air and practiced – "I love you sweetheart." Almost everyone had done that. Also, they looked at each other and blushed.

Sitting on the tree top platforms, Mansoor, Akbar, Murid and Kazi looked down at the shooting. They found it hilarious. They had finished drinking bottles of wine and whiskey. The empty bottles were lying around them. They had no idea what was going on? Was it a dream or real?

Their attention wasn't at the narrow road or the helicopter passing overhead. They enjoyed watching Mushtaq, Tipu, Salim, Omar and many others doing the act.

Iqbal encouraged Jabbar and told him to breathe in and breathe out, relax and do it.

Mansoor saw something unusual, he showed Abbas, Changez, Kadar, Murid and Kazi. They were shocked to see Mushtaq and Chandni practice the lines and hug each other. They were jealous. Why were girls friendly with Mushtaq?

Jabbar was tired. The moment Crystal touched him he got distracted & messed up his lines.

Mastani and Mallika couldn't stop laughing. They, for the moment had forgotten that Jabbar Ellahi was a terrorist who had accepted the challenge of this job.

Jabbar jumbled his words, "I kick you like earth and make you football. I will melt myself to mountain."

"I love you and …." He forgot. Each time Crystal's hug would blow him out of his mind. Crystal realized what was happening.

Everyone in the movie unit thought it's a futile exercise except one person– Iqbal. He was still confident that Jabbar would make it.

Iqbal decided to take a break. Crystal suggested that they should practice alone in Jabbar's den.

"Can I practice with him in his den?" Crystal asked.

"Ask him if he agrees." Iqbal too thought it might work.

"We should try all possibilities." Shweta seconded the idea.

"Let's take a break and relax for some time." Iqbal announced.

Jabbar headed to his den and Crystal followed him. Jabbar knew she was coming. He pretended to be unaware of her walking in.

Crystal was looking for a place where they can sit.

"Sit here." Jabber offered the big rock where he used to sit.

"No. That is your place." Crystal refused politely and respectfully to the blue-eyed boy.

"Be my guest please." Jabbar said with utter politeness and respect, pulling a plastic chair for himself.

"It isn't as easy as I thought." He confessed.

"It's very easy Beb." Crystal smiled, "Just relax and sip your coffee."

"Beb?" Jabbar asked, "Who is Beb?"

"You. Your short form." She smiled.

"I am Jabbar Ellahi. You can call me JE, that is my short form."

"No. I will call you BEB. Blue Eyed Boy." Crystal praised him.

Crystal's googly hit the middle wicket. He was out for pavilion. Jabbar didn't know what to say. He blushed and his face turned red. She was hitting on him.

She continued, "You look like a Hollywood hero."

"Really, you think so?" He felt shy, but great, as the compliment was coming from Crystal.

"Have you ever touched a woman before? Did you have a girlfriend?" Crystal asked. Jabbar found that so bizarre.

"Never. Why?"

"Just like that. It's very important to know each other if we are working together."

"Hmm." Jabbar looked at her beautiful innocent face, "Are you from Kashmir?"

"Himachal, I am from Manali. I live in Mumbai now. But I go and meet my parents every now and then. They like peaceful Manali."

"You are from Manali?" Jabbar got excited and spoke in a high-pitched voice, "Last year I was hiding there with my group. Police and military both were looking for us. We traveled in an old bus. The bus driver was from Kashmir, he helped us reach Manali.

We took shelter for many weeks there. Locals helped us, they fed us and took care of us. I am very happy to know that you are from my place. Manali and Kashmir are neighbors."

"Really!" Crystal showed the same excitement, she hugged him & said, "We are neighbors."

Both Jabbar Ellahi and Crystal chatted about Manali and Srinagar.

"Can I smoke if you don't mind?" Jabbar asked.

"Why should I? Please go ahead."

Jabbar took out his weed packet, rolled it in paper and lit it.

"Roll one for me too." Crystal looked at it and said.

Jabbar was shocked out of his wits when he heard that request from cute and innocent looking girl. He recalled Iqbal saying, "It was common in Bollywood."

That's fine! It might be common in Bollywood. Men used to smoke this but Crystal? She too smoked this? I guess yes, she asked for it. She wanted it.

"It's marijuana." Jabbar hesitated.

"I know what it is."

Jabbar rolled a joint. He lit it, took a couple of drags and passed it on to Crystal. Jabbar and Crystal both smoked it together.

CHAPTER 16

When the entire nation was drowning in sorrow and worry, when the government of India was trying to locate the terrorists, media and social media had just one topic Iqbal and Jabbar Ellahi, the Indian film industry was brain storming on how to tackle the situation, when Aditya Raghuvanshi and Javed Khan were busy cracking information and the PM was losing sleep over the abduction... Jabbar Ellahi was busy reading lines with hot Crystal. The terrorist leader was preparing for the shot with Crystal. They smoked and felt light and relaxed. Jabbar was fully charged to prove that he could act in films too. It was not a big deal. The big deal was only to free Kashmir. He knew he would do it one day, come what may.

Jabbar was impressed with Crystal. A diva who came from Manali and made a name for herself in the cut throat competition of Bollywood where every day, youngsters land in hundreds, with silver dreams in their eyes. Only a handful get success. Most return to their villages and some make do with small odd jobs.

Crystal was a star. Jabbar was a newcomer, learning his lines.

"Let's practice now." Jabbar offered.

He was somebody who would never give up. Crystal liked his spirit.

***

Jabbar Ellahi came out looking confident with Crystal and looked at the unit, "Let's do it now."

Iqbal stood up. The film unit was at work in less than a minute. Mushtaq was amazed at their efficiency.

One command from Iqbal, "Are we ready for the take?"

Everyone was ready and alert to do their best.

Jabbar was very focused too. He delivered.

He did everything perfectly– in one go. He hugged Crystal without any hesitation as if he knew her for ages. Everyone clapped. Mushtaq was the first to congratulate him.

"Wonderful Bhai! You have done it."

Iqbal gave him a few more lines and described the scene. Jabbar did it effortlessly. The shooting continued till lunch without a hitch.

***

Lunch time was flirting time for some pairs- Mushtaq and Chandni, Salim and Mallika and Mastani and Tipu. The singles– Abbas, Bilal, Changez, Kadar, Abrar, were still searching for girls they could strike up a conversation with.

Abbas and Bilal caught Mastani when she was going to the vanity van. She was alone. They grabbed her. They lifted her and took her behind the vanity van. There was some space between two buses. They found the place suitable. Mastani was struggling and tried screaming but Abbas had his hand on her mouth. She couldn't do anything. They threatened her.

"We will kill you if you scream," Abbas said and put her down on the grass. Bilal was holding her legs. Abbas pulled her top. His ugly bearded face without mustache looked like an animal who was ready to kill its pray and devour. She was helpless and vulnerable. Abbas saw her topless body and took his hand to his pant to remove it. They forgot for a moment that Mansoor, Akbar, Murid, Kazi were watching them from the top. They whistled and signaled Tipu. Tipu was shocked to see them. He took out his gun.

"Leave her." He pointed his gun at the duo.

"Why? Only you will have fun? What about us?" Abbas said and realized Mushtaq, Omar & Salim had come and stood behind Tipu.

Mastani got up and covered herself. She was shaken and sobbing.

Before they could say anything Jabbar appeared out of nowhere. He stood in front of them. He looked at them. He slapped Abbas and Bilal.

"How dare you?" Bilal was silent. Abbas bowed his hand. Mastani was weeping, she stood behind Jabbar. "We are freedom fighters and not rapists." Jabbar said and left.

***

Inside the den all the culprits were standing in front of Jabbar Ellahi with their heads hung in shame. Jabbar's eyes were burning red with anger. No one dared to look up at Jabbar. Jabbar would never tolerate this kind of nonsense.

"Mushtaq, Omar and Salim started that. They also did the same..." Bilal complained.

"Is that true Mushtaq?"

"Ask if any girl speaks against us, I will shoot myself." Mushtaq replied immediately, "We were trying to understand things from them so that we can convert them and bring them on our side." Mushtaq was clever.

"Right! We have to make them comfortable." Omar supported Mushtaq, "So that they join us. It was Bhai's order and we were following that order."

Jabbar was satisfied with the reply.

"Next time if any such thing happens you will be dead." Jabbar looked in to Abbas's eyes. Abbas and Bilal were quiet.

CHAPTER 17

Rawalpindi, Pakistan.

Qamar Javed Bajwa, Pakistan's army chief, relaxed after a hectic meeting. He asked his lunch to be served. He was keeping an eye on Kashmir's activities. Bajwa was the most powerful man in Pakistan. He flexed his muscle whenever he needed and twisted Imran's arm when he showed attitude or ignored him. Whether its US government or Chinese establishment Bajwa had to be taken in confidence before taking decisions. They ran this nation, not the elected government which had credibility in the public eye. This country needed dictatorship anyway, democracy was just a façade. It was a big responsibility to run a country like this which has faced debacles one after another, whether it was India or East Pakistan. Till the time Congress was in rule they bullied Indians with terrorism.

But the new Indian government was challenging. They were not just quick to react with surgical strikes but they were proactive. This

PM believed in throwing surprises at them. He had made Pakistani establishment and army restless. They had removed Article 370 and now were eyeing POK. Pakistani army was alert 24x7.

Imran repeatedly reminded the world that all this happened because of radical actions of the present PM of India. Imran predicted war and added that both the countries were nuclear power. He requested the international community to intervene as it is inhumane to impose curfew for so many months in J&K. No one supported him, no one paid attention to what Imran urged.

Bajwa didn't know when, what would come from India. The PM was decisive and did surgical strike inside their territory and all they could do was to watch and complain. No one paid heed to him. India was aggressive this time. They had to be very careful, they could fight a proxy war with India, but war with India? No way. No one would support a country like Pak, no one at all.

The abduction of 370 people was good news for Pakistan after a long time.

Bajwa knew India's present government wouldn't sit idle. The entire machinery had got an impetus and a sensible solution was getting cracked. Imran Khan made a statement that they had nothing to do with the abduction of innocent film crew.

"There would be bloodbath once the curfew is lifted." Imran Khan toured America, London and Europe asking for help. No one bought his argument. A few reminded him of 9/11. The media questioned his integrity when it came to fighting terrorism.

Imran came back, "I am disappointed with the international community. Kashmiri Muslims are suffering because of an autocratic Hitler like Prime Minister of India who let Muslims be butchered in Gujrat during his tenure as CM."

Imran Khan explained in his media conferences about Islam, "Islam is the only religion which we practice in our day to day lives. He quoted a movie he watched when he was in London (as a student) - a movie which mocked Christ. This couldn't be done with Islam. Muslims would not take this kind of attack. He then talked about Salman Rushdie's book -The Satanic Verses.

He tried to convince the Pakistani army that he was doing his best. However, Pakistani army clearly stated that 'Your best is not good enough. Attack India with a nuclear bomb.'

Imran discussed the problem in a very confidential one on one meeting with army chief Qamar Javed, "War with India will wipe out Pakistan from the world map. This man is deadly. No one is with us, not even China. You know the reality of China. Their interest is in trade and land. To tell you the truth China is our real enemy, not India." He sighed and continued with his usual nose poking habit, "They keep Muslims in refugee camps like animals and treat them like slaves."

Bajwa listened patiently, "Tell me something I don't know. All I want to do is to keep talking about war. That's it. Let the videos boil on social media. It would keep Pakistani's calm." He spoke like a seasoned politician. He knew Imran was a kid in politics and knew nothing more than cricket. A womanizer was made a Prime Minister. His ex-wife wrote a book and ripped his secret sexual relationships. Bloody homosexual! He hated him. He just knew how to talk. It is unfortunate for Pakistan that a man like him was the PM.

Bajwa had a series of meetings with him. Imran was often arrogant and started preaching without any real understanding of issues. He hardly understood Pakistan. Bajwa was fed up but didn't show his frustration in front of the PM. He pursued his meetings with Hafiz Saeed who had muscle power and people who were ready to avenge India.

Hafiz managed to provoke people against Imran and brought a crowd of almost a million people on the roads of Pakistan for more than 48 hours. Imran panicked. He saw his PM chair slipping from under him. He immediately contacted Bajwa for reconciliation. Hafiz was offered his share of meat to normalize the situation.

He waited to hear some good news from Shabbir after his man Jabbar Ellahi abducted a movie crew of 370 people.

"Hafiz Saab is here to see you" orderly informed Bajwa. He was irked, *without any prior appointment?* "Take him to the conference room," he replied after few thoughtful seconds. He got up to meet Hafiz. Both of them disliked Imran but there was a difference between them. Bajwa was a general, a sophisticated army officer and Hafiz was a terrorist. Both of them were licensed to kill innocent people for their own vested interest and both took orders from USA and China. Bajwa was hesitant to meet him openly and frequently, especially in his office in broad day-light.

Hafiz with two men entered the conference room. Long white kurta, loose pajama and a black-and-white checkered scarf, like the one Yasar Arafat used to have, long cruel face with a long beard without mustache. He drank water offered by the office peon.

"Salam walekum," Hafiz greeted him first.

"Walekum Salam," Bajwa responded and looked at the other two men with Hafiz.

"There is something wrong with the communication." Hafiz started the conversation without any background, "I need to contact Shabbir, do you know whose pawn is Jabbar?"

Bajwa looked at his two men sitting beside him.

"Don't worry. They are with me." He sounded too authoritative for Bajwa's liking.

"We will wait outside." One of them understood Bajwa's discomfort. They left the room.

There was silence for a moment, Bajwa recalled his query. "Absolutely no idea, this fellow, Jabbar is Shabbir's baby, he has trained him. Indian army is on red alert, may be that's the reason he wasn't taking your calls." Bajwa cautioned him, "We need to be prepared for any mishap."

"I have a plan to divert the Indian army"

"At this very hour we should wait for the international community's reaction, my digital team is busy making the video viral. Imagine what would happen after these 370 people die?"

"Will Indian government fall?" Hafiz questioned.

"Do you think so?" Bajwa was apprehensive, "Military would go mad rather."

"Wouldn't they get a huge message about Kashmir?"

"Yes, the entire world is discussing Kashmir today."

"Shabbir's party may have minted tonnes of money." Hafiz was jealous.

"Massive amount of money, he deserves that." Bajwa hinted that Hafiz had missed an opportunity, his plan of abducting 370 people wasn't simple." He praised Shabbir and implied that Hafiz should have done something like that.

"I am planning to send few men to blast the valley which will keep them engaged."

"Not a good idea." He discouraged him, "We should wait and watch the Indian government. Modi is unpredictable, let's not play on the forefront."

"I am being pressurized by Syrians."

"Go ahead if you want."

"We need some ammunition, can we…?"

Oh! That's the reason this bugger was here! He needed ammunition. For what? To sell it to others?

"I have to discuss with my team."

"Don't share this with the psycho." He winked and laughed; his big belly shook like a jelly. He looked like a monster and he was a monster, wanted by many countries. He was protected by Bajwa. He operated terrorist camps, appointed unemployed youth on the path of no return. Bajwa needed him. If he had to survive in Pakistan, he had to survive with these sorts of men.

Bajwa knew who he meant. He didn't want to have their conversation shared with Imran Khan. Imran knew nothing about these deals, only army had the knowledge.

The discussion went on for a long time. Bajwa wanted to have his share before he gave army's ammunition to Hafiz.

"I will let you know, let this be settled first." Bajwa postponed the deal for the time being.

"Do you mean Jabbar's issue?"

"This issue has taken the world by storm. We are watching it closely." Bajwa clarified.

People like Hafiz were useful at times, Bajwa knew how to use a terrorist head like him.

***

Shabbir Mallik & Muneer Lone both lit their cigars and pulled the smoke in their lungs. The expensive nicotine helped them think deeply about Jabbar Ellahi. He called all his friends in Dubai, Syria, London and Pakistan. He ignored Hafiz's call. He was in touch with Bajwa.

They congratulated him, wished him all the best for his freedom fight for Kashmir. They wanted to know when the killings will happen. But the ball was in Jabbar's court and all they could do was to wait for him to act.

Jabbar played smart and didn't give the Indian government any opportunity to get into action. The politician couldn't take a chance and jeopardize 370 Indian lives. Especially when they had no idea about the location- whether it was in India or Pakistan.

They still couldn't figure out how and why Jabbar changed so much, so suddenly.

"Something is wrong with Jabbar. Something is cooking; don't you think?" Muneer suspected, "Is Jabbar telling you the truth?"

Shabbir didn't deny it. He was quiet. He knew Muneer was right but he dared not voice it.

"He is taking decisions. That's it. He is with us but wants to be more powerful." Shabbir reassured him. If Jabbar crossed his limits, he would be cut down to size. It happened in politics all the time. People crossed lines and needed some eye opening.

"I will cut Jabbar down to size. I am waiting for the right time," Shabbir spoke. He knew the ball would be in his court soon. It was a matter of time. He will dictate terms with Jabbar then.

Lone smiled, "They have limited rations up on the hill top."

"Now you got it." Shabbir smiled.

"I provide everything to Jabbar and his team. Now they have extra 370 people eating. Either he had to kill them all or call Rehman for rations." Shabbir pulled a puff smiling cunningly, "If he kills them, army will react and kill Jabbar Ellahi and his men. We would announce immediately that Jabbar Ellahi is alive, appointing a new man as Jabbar Ellahi." Mallik had a plan ready, "We will send a new video with new masked Jabbar Ellahi!"

"What if he asks for provisions?" Lone raised his query.

"I will make him realize that I am the Boss." Mallik pulled another puff, "Jabbar would then come to his knees."

***

Chhatrapati Shivaji Airport, Mumbai.

Rahim Akhtar & Ayesha Alam walked on shining white ceramic floors. Everything glittered in the fancy lights. It looked like a five-star hotel. It said India wasn't a poor country at all. Here farmers committed suicide every year. Media reported the numbers. Indians listened to it and continued their day-today lives. It wasn't a big deal for them. All of that just vanished with the opulence around.

They came out of the airport, both walked in to Starbucks.

"Coffee?" He looked at Ayesha.

The girl at the counter looked at him, "How many, sir?"

"I will have one." Rahim said without looking at Ayesha, "Americano black coffee." Rahim placed his order. Ayesha didn't like his attitude. He was a typical Kashmiri man. No respect for women.

"One Americano for me too." Ayesha placed her own order.

She liked black coffee.

"What name would you like to be called once the coffee is ready?" The girl asked.

"Rahim."

"Ayesha."

Both said at the same time. Rahim turned around like a robot and sat on a chair. Ayesha followed him and pulled a chair opposite him.

They sat and waited silently for their names to be called.

Rahim slept through the flight as usual. That was the only 'me time' he got on business trips. He hardly spoke anyway!

Ayesha was a hot Kashmiri babe. People looked at her. *This guy was different, he had attitude.*

"How should we go about it?" Ayesha started the conversation.

"I have a friend here, Rahul Chandra. He will give us contacts. We will call the actors and directors who knew Iqbal, take their views and send to Shekhar immediately."

"Rahim, Ayesha" the girl called their names.

Both went and picked up their own coffee.

"You hardly speak." Ayesha complained while sipping her coffee.

"I have got a headache."

His curt reply was a hint for her to shut up. She silently sipped her coffee.

"I am pained with Kashmir's situation. There is no fresh air left to breathe. People live in bitterness." He started a conversation. He might have realized his rudeness. Ayesha decided to participate in the conversation, "Everyone is scared of arrests. Almost all the leaders of Kashmir have been arrested."

"Yup, they have made a mockery of democracy. We all watch like jokers." Rahim kept the coffee mug on the table, "I don't enjoy reporting. I feel I am one of those spectators who sit back and watch. I follow Mayank's instructions. Shekhar takes orders from New Delhi. Everyone is for sale- with a price tag." He paused. He looked around at the luxury.

"Our people have failed us." Rahim felt dejected.

He was again lost in thought, as always. Rahim was a serious journalist and Ayesha respected him professionally. He had soft fair, bearded face and he didn't look like a tough crime reporter. His full lips and bushy eyebrows were really attractive.

***

Ayesha and Rahim interviewed Lalwani.

Lalwani was worried about what would happen to his movie if Iqbal and the crew members were killed. He blamed the army and police for negligence of duty. He himself was to go for the shooting. Fortunately, he was held up and was safe.

The report was sent to Mayank.

"Let's go to FTII Pune. Iqbal studied there."

"How far is Pune from here?" Ayesha asked.

"It would take us four hours to reach Pune."

They left for Pune after a quick lunch.

CHAPTER 18

Abbas, Bilal, Changez, Kadar and Abrar were planning to sabotage Jabbar.

"He didn't give us wine and vodka, only a few brandy bottles." Abrar had his own grievance.

"Mushtaq is a mad dog and mad dogs need to be shot dead." Abbas was very upset with Mushtaq.

"We have to contact Shabbir Bhai." Kadar initiated.

"Against Jabbar Bhai? He will kill us the moment he gets to know." Abrar warned them.

"He is nothing without Shabbir Bhai's support. Don't forget. He doesn't know what is happening here. This song and dance are against Islam," Abbas said firmly, "He is a changed guy now. I bet he has fallen in love with that chic- the heroine."

Changez supported him, "Yes, he was supposed to do just one scene. Now he is shooting scene after scene."

"What is going on here is not good." Bilal supported them, "I am not with Jabbar, we have been debarred from girls and they enjoy them."

Five of them, Abbas, Bilal, Changez, Kadar, Abrar decided on mutiny against Jabbar Ellahi.

"We will contact Shabbir Bhai when he is busy shooting."

***

Lunch time was over. Iqbal asked Aman to call for 'break over'.

The call was made, "Break over."

Iqbal was preparing for the next scene.

Crystal changed her costume. She looked prettier in a white salwar and deep necked red kurti. She wore big round earnings and let her silky black hair open. She went to Jabbar to practice the scene. Jabbar looked at her and smiled without uttering a word. She smiled back.

It was a long scene. They rehearsed.

Iqbal called them once the shot was ready.

"You have to walk from here to that point. There is a mark where you have to stop and turn. Crystal will be here already. You catch her hand, climb to the mound and finish the rest of your lines. Stop right on this mark. The steady cam will move with you. It will follow you from the back and move to cover you from the front." Iqbal explained the shot.

"What is a steady cam?" Jabbar asked.

Iqbal showed the equipment that held the camera on it. It moved with actor's movement covering all the activities.

Jabbar rehearsed the scene and was ready to go for a take. Iqbal and the whole unit were stunned to see his performance. Jabbar waited for Iqbal to say 'Cut'. Iqbal was so engrossed that he forgot to say 'Cut'. For a moment no one spoke. They clapped for Jabbar.

Jabbar walked to his den when everyone was still clapping. He didn't realize his eyes were wet suddenly. Tears were rolling down his cheeks. *Why? What had happened? Because of the love and acceptance of the film crew? Was it because of the appreciation?* He had never felt so honored ever before. That was a different experience.

He was emotional because he encountered something which was due for long. He had struggled all his life. He missed Ammi after a long time. He had become so hard and cold. Negativity and brutal thoughts had made him ruthless. He was now getting back to his original self. *What about the freedom of Kashmir? Allah knows that.* He thought. *Allah wanted him to be a freedom fighter. He fought for Kashmir. And would do it in future. Let Allah order his next course of action, he was ready for that.* He wiped his tears as Crystal entered the den.

She came in and hugged him.

"You are a great artist Blue eyed boy."

Jabbar blushed.

Crystal noticed his tears. She knew they were tears of joy.

Iqbal called him for the next shot. He was ready to deliver as the hero of the movie *Azadi*.

Jabbar shot with Iqbal the whole day till the sunset.

After sunset Iqbal, Jabbar, Crystal, Shweta, Mushtaq, Tipu sat around the bonfire and enjoyed tea and munchies.

***

Abbas, Bilal, Changez, Kadar, Abrar met near the den. They found the time right to inform Shabbir Mallik.

"Wait outside and whistle if someone comes here." Abbas ordered them. They dispersed and stood outside the den.

Abbas called Shabbir. He didn't pick up the phone. Abbas was scared. He would be shot dead if anyone knew he called Shabbir.

Shabbir picked up the call when Abbas dialed again.

"Bhai Adaab, I am Abbas calling. Here things are not good. Jabbar has gone mad. He is flirting with the heroine and he has become a hero here. Shooting is going on since morning."

Shabbir couldn't believe his ears. "What did you say?"

"Jabbar is having fun with girls. He is dancing and shooting that movie."

What happened to his man? He was shooting? Had he gone mad? Shabbir thought.

"Jabbar, Mushtaq, Tipu, Salim are all busy having fun here. I can't talk for long. I want to meet you."

"You come and meet me tonight at Rehman's place." He instructed him.

Shabbir was shocked. *What was this? His dog had crossed the line.*

He understood why Jabbar had changed his plans.

***

The day slipped in to evening turning the sky into a brilliant canvas of dusky hues.

Kabir headed to manage dinner for the crew with the help of his assistants Raman & Pancham. He kept everything ready for Rambabu -Shayambabu. They had limited supplies with them. Mushtaq had got the stuff from his store in a big tempo.

The weather was chilly. Omar, Salim and Tipu started a bon fire. Spot boys Guddu, Babloo, Rafee and Pankaj helped make dinner. They served coffee and snacks to Jabbar, Crystal, Mastani, Mallika, Iqbal, Shweta and Chandni who were warming themselves in front of the fire.

Jabbar gave a shawl to Crystal.

"Last month when I was in Pahalgam, it was gifted to me. It will keep you warm." Jabbar was kind hearted. Crystal realized. She met a terrorist for the first time in her life. He was no different than the others. He never insulted her. He cried like a baby when appreciated. He was just like them.

"You are very kind." Crystal was very moved by the gesture.

"We all are kind. We love our land, that is our only fault." Jabbar sighed, "We are freedom fighters."

"I saw your eyes well up when everyone applauded your performance." Iqbal extended both his arms closer to the burning fire for warmth.

"I don't know why and how it happened." Jabbar accepted it whole heartedly.

"We sacrifice years for that kind of appreciation. Those claps are actually love. They keep us going and inspire us to work harder." Iqbal was serious when he said that, "Trust me, the entire world will love you. They would laugh and cry in the theatre with you. Cinema engages you. It helps you grow your intellect and personality. You know why people watch cinema? It relaxes them and distracts them from the hustle of their mundane life. People will fall sick without cinema or entertainment. Cinema has that magic. It's a complete medication. Another world altogether." Iqbal talked from his heart.

"Your fans would like to know everything about you. What you like, don't like. Where you were born, about your parents, your girlfriend, even what kind of food you like. They want to connect with you. They follow your hairstyles, fashions and copy whatever you do. You will be the hero of their lives." Iqbal stopped and looked at Crystal, "She is a big star. Ask her. People go crazy to get one glimpse of her. There would be a traffic jam if they got to know that she is traveling on that route. Crystal can't walk on the road just like that."

Crystal blushed. She was overwhelmed with emotion and gratitude.

"Yes, I have seen her film posters, photos and videos on social media. We post our mission quotations on Facebook. I saw her film trailer popping up." Jabbar suddenly recalled her. "But when I saw her for the first time, I didn't recognize her. You look different on screen." Then Jabbar said something which made Crystal feel good. "Your parents must be worried about you."

Crystal suddenly faced the reality of the situation. There was silence for a while. No one spoke.

Jabbar Ellahi didn't like the talk of cinema. He was doing it because this film was about freedom- *Azadi*. Otherwise he was the last one to be interested in these idiotic, futile exercises.

"But I am not made for acting or stardom," Jabbar said with a heavy heart, "My purpose is Kashmir's freedom," Jabbar was determined, "Iqbal, don't forget that I am doing this film only because you are making this film on our culture and freedom of Kashmir."

"Of course!" Iqbal supported it. "Freedom is the foundation. Only if you have a free mind can you do anything. An enslaved mind can't love anyone or anything."

Jabbar didn't understand Iqbal's logic for love. The only love Jabbar knew was for his motherland Kashmir.

"We have to think about Kashmir Iqbal," Jabbar was direct, "Let me know who all are with us and ready to fight for Kashmir's freedom. Those who are not with us would be killed and their bodies sent to New Delhi." Jabbar was serious.

There was a tense silence. Jabbar was a tough nut to crack.

***

Iqbal was disappointed with Jabbar. He was so adamant. Iqbal knew he was brainwashed by ruthless people with ulterior motives.

Jabbar knew no other way but to kill or be killed for Kashmir. He had crossed the line & couldn't go back and change his past. Once a terrorist, always a terrorist.

He had cast Jabbar Ellahi in his film. A terrorist who fought for Kashmir. What would happen to him if public knew that his lead actor was a terrorist?

He would be branded as a traitor. Bollywood, politicians, public- no one will spare him. They will shout slogans against him. This government was greatly into slogans – for every scheme, event and of course elections.

Iqbal was approached to write slogans for a political party. He was offered a handsome remuneration for it. Bansi Pandey (Power Broker) offered the job, "They would pay you well- much better than well."

"This is only for the election period, right?" Iqbal asked.

"Political parties will need you from time and again. Slogans make or break a government in democracy. Slogans keep people calm and they are assured that something is happening or would happen. Fresh innovative slogans are the need of the hour." Bansi Pandey explained. Iqbal remembered; each government had a slogan.

"They may fund your movie if they like your slogan. You know in this economic crisis where no one has money, only politicians can invest." Bansi lured Iqbal with another offer. He knew his interest was movies and not slogans. He knew Iqbal was creative and could write good slogans.

"No harm in writing slogans. Let's try our luck." Shweta was for taking up the offer.

Before Iqbal could get cracking on the slogans, government revoked Article 370 and Lalwani called him to start this film.

***

Iqbal was pondering. What if Lalwani lodged a case against him? According to the contract he could not replace Prabhas or Crystal.

"Lalwani would rip you apart." Shweta put it mildly, "He has the money, power and goons. He wouldn't go to the court or police. He has his own army for people like you." Shweta joked.

Iqbal was scared of Shweta's joke turning in to a reality. This project had gotten way too complex. He didn't know a way out.

The movie was shaping up well and was hyped internationally.

Lalwani was a businessman- he would not be unhappy. Rather he would appreciate it. He had saved all. His film *Azadi* would be a big hit. He was sure about it.

Jabbar suited the role. If he continued shooting the movie, 370 people will survive, else everyone would die. Iqbal had his plans and Jabbar had his own plans too.

No one knew what Jabbar's plans were.

CHAPTER 19

Dinner was peaceful. Everyone relished the delicious food. Jabbar dined with the team. He complimented the cooks. The bonfire had kept everyone warm. Crystal and Jabbar talked for a long time.

"I won't forget these beautiful moments all my life." Crystal said looking at Jabbar, "I never have enjoyed dinner under an open sky."

"You will remember only the dinner under open sky or …" Jabbar whispered.

Crystal smiled. She knew what he meant.

"What about you? Wouldn't you miss our company." Crystal asked.

"Till the time I live, I will live with these memories." Jabbar looked into her eyes. She blushed.

Jabbar called Mushtaq after dinner.

"It's very cold outside. Crystal and other girls can sleep in the den." Jabbar tilted his neck to look at Mushtaq, "Rest of the girls can sleep in vanity van and bus."

"Where will you sleep?" Mushtaq asked.

"You know I hardly sleep. We all can sleep under the tin sheds." Jabbar looked far away in the darkness and was lost in thoughts.

Mushtaq realized that Jabbar had changed. Had he fallen in love with Crystal?

He saw Chandni. He waved at her. She waved back.

***

Rahim and Ayesha reached Pune around 5:00 PM. They rushed to FTII (Film & Television Institute of India) for an interview. They met FTII director Krishnan Acharya. A stout man with long white hair and a white flowing beard. His big wide nose had thick glass lenses sitting on it. He adorned long Kurta and loose trousers. Krishnan had a complete intellectual look.

"Iqbal was a very bright student. He had a great career ahead of him." The director was unhappy with the government, "We will go to Delhi with our students and march to the PMO soon. It is the responsibility of the government to keep us safe."

"What according to you would be an appropriate step at this moment?" Rahim asked.

"The government of the day should think. They are running the country, not us." Krishnan was a little upset with the question, "You should ask this question to your ministers, not us."

Rahim Akhtar looked at him.

"Don't you think we all need to voice our opinions about Article 370." Ayesha asked.

"We should do a lot many things. We would do anything and everything to save Iqbal and movie crew." Krishnan replied.

"So criticizing the government would help?" Ayesha asked again, "What has your institution done, except appealing and criticizing- if I may ask?"

"We have all the right to condemn and criticize the government, which we have done and will continue doing; so that government doesn't fall asleep." He said firmly.

FTII was a government institution and Krishnan had survived as a director of the institute despite being a communist. He always spoke against the government but hadn't been replaced.

Politicians knew that if he was not given any post, he would create trouble. To shut him up they appointed him as the director.

***

Rahim and Ayesha sent the full interview to Rudra Shekhar.

"Have you met Samar Nakhate?" Asked Shekhar, "Meet him, you must! He is very popular in Pune as a freelance teacher."

Rahim had heard this name before. "We will try and meet Samar Nakhate too." replied a tired Rahim. *How did Shekhar know about him? Was he in touch with people here too? Shekhar was very resourceful and vibrant, that's why he was the editor-in-chief for so many years.*

They walked on Deccan Gymkhana road to find a restaurant for chai and snacks. They saw students waving to a man in khaki pajama kurta and a cloth *shabnam* bag on his shoulder. He was smiling, waving back to students cheerfully.

"Who is he?" Ayesha asked the waiter who was taking their order.

"Samar Nakhate." The waiter replied and guessed, "You are new here!"

Rahim didn't say a word. "Let's go catch him first." Rahim stood up and headed towards Samar Nakhate. Ayesha followed him.

"May I have a few minutes Sir?" Rahim shouted. Samar Nakhate stopped and turned back to see who was chasing him. He smiled. He had a whitish, calm face. His smile made his persona unique. You want just a few minutes? I can give you hours if you want"

"Thanks a ton!" Ayesha smiled back, "We are from Kashmir covering abduction of the film crew…"

Soon Rahim, Ayesha, and Nakhate were in Symbiosis college canteen. The waiter served them ginger tea and bun butter.

"Iqbal is very close to me; he was one of those brilliant students. He always wished to make films for global audience. He has superb survival instincts. He had called me when he got the project, he was thrilled," Nakhate sighed, "It is sad what happened to his film unit."

"Tell us about Iqbal. Was he religious?" Ayesha was curious.

"His approach was humane rather than religious. He never believed in any one religion. His stories dealt with human suffering. He was spiritual, read all religious books – Bible, Geeta, Ramayana, Sufism, Jainism, Quran. He was very well-read, especially interested in life and death. He has written unique stories that dealt with human emotions and existential stuff."

Samar Nakhate was humble and friendly. They loved his company. Ayesha recoded his interview on her mobile phone camera. Then he had got a call from someone, "I have to meet a group of students. I am here. Call me anytime for any information." He left hurriedly.

"What a beautiful place." Rahim looked at the hills. Ayesha called Shekhar to confirm that he got her footage.

"Yup, got it! We will telecast it soon."

Rahim and Ayesha got out of the canteen. They needed a place to stay. They looked for a hotel close by. They entered the first hotel they found at Prabhat road JW Marriott.

"Only one room is available," the receptionist said looking at them; as if they didn't take that room, it would be taken soon.

"Please book that room," Ayesha said immediately.

***

The waiter showed them the room. Kept a complimentary water bottle and a basket of fruits. He glanced at Ayesha and left after asking if they needed anything.

Rahim took out his cigarette packet, picked out one and lit it. He didn't bother asking Ayesha if she was okay with him smoking or not.

"Can I have one?" Ayesha asked.

Rahim passed the cigarette pack to her. She took one out and lit it. She wanted to start the conversation but Rahim didn't look interested.

Ayesha smoked quietly and went to take a shower. She came out of the shower wearing a pair of black tights and a kurti.

"Dinner?" Ayesha looked at him and smiled. She knew he was unpredictable. Rahim went to the washroom and came out wearing polo T-shirt on the same pair of denims.

Both headed for the inhouse restaurant.

***

"You did well. You could be a good reporter," Rahim was a bit patronizing.

"Meaning? I am not good now?"

"Practice makes you perfect. Experience is required. Everyone needs it. You are no exception." Rahim looked in to her eyes for the first time.

Their friendship started shaping up with that dinner. Ayesha felt he paid attention to her.

Ayesha switched on the TV and found Samar Nakhate's interview was being aired on Valley news. She watched it with Rahim.

"I appeal to those who want to retaliate and take revenge. Killing innocent people will invite immense problems for everyone. Draconian law- 'eye for an eye' justice wouldn't work. It would just make the whole world blind. This blood bath will take them nowhere, also, Iqbal is a filmmaker who respects all… So, my only request to them is to end it. Violence has no place in solving any problem…"

Rahim's phone rang, it was Shekhar, "I got great response, good job!" Shekhar sounded happy, "Get some students' response tomorrow based on Nakhate's interview."

"Will do that."

They spoke for a quite some time. Ayesha kept watching the interview.

They crashed in one large bed, maintaining a safe distance between them.

***

2:00 AM midnight.

Aditya got up with an incessant ring of his phone. He took it.

"Shabbir has come out. He is driving his own car and has a someone with him." Sunder Iyer, his commander, was reporting.

"Ok." He hung up and quickly got dressed.

Shabbir's activities were under strict surveillance. Aditya arrived at the check post.

Shabbir's black SUV was stopped by the army and checked thoroughly.

"Where are you headed?" Aditya asked Shabbir. "I am going to meet someone who works for me. He is not well."

"You have no doctor with you."

"The doctor is reaching directly to his place." Shabbir smiled.

"Let him go." Aditya smiled back.

The barrier was lifted.

Aditya called Javed, "Shabbir is on the move. Tracker has been fixed." "Okay. I will monitor him."

***

Rehman was awake and waiting for Shabbir. He took him inside and offered him a chair.

"Should I make some coffee?"

"No. I am good."

"It's cold outside." Shabbir ignored Rehman.

"What time he said he would be here?" Asked Shabbir

"Any moment …"

Rehman heard some noise. He went outside and came back with Abbas. Rehman handed him a water bottle.

"Adab Bhai!" Abbas greeted.

Rehman left them alone to talk.

"Only Allah knows what Jabbar is up to. He has shaved his beard and wears jeans –T shirt, he spends time with Crystal- that famous heroine." Abbas drank water from the bottle.

"Hmm!" Shabbir looked worried, "What's the plan? Is he not going to kill them?"

"Never. He is just passing time with the heroine." Abbas complained, "Mushtaq, Tipu, Salim and all flirt with the girls. When we tried to complain, Mushtaq objected. He complained to Jabbar. Jabbar threatened us to kill us if we touch any girl as we are freedom fighters. Only Jabbar can touch and flirt with girls, not us."

Shabbir understood the root of Abbas's anger. He was not given a chance to have fun with the girls. Smile gripped Shabbir's lips. He knew now how to play his game.

"They are all yours. Do whatever you want to do. You and your friends have a free hand to take a call on who lives and who dies. You will be the next Jabbar Ellahi."

"But how is it possible when Jabbar Ellahi is alive?"

"We have a plan for that. I will call Jabbar here," Shabbir sighed, "I will ask Jabbar to come down and meet me with the director of the film. He is viral on social media ever since Jabbar sent the video."

"Iqbal?"

"Yes Iqbal." He repeated his name and continued sharing his plan "You stay back there with your trusted men. Jabbar always moves with Mushtaq, Omar, Salim, and Tipu. Rehman and my men will take care of them," He paused for a moment, "They would definitely come down but won't go back."

"I will never ditch you like Jabbar." Abbas assured him, "I will always obey your orders."

"You are Jabbar Ellahi now." Shabbir assured him.

"Kashmir will be a free nation. Inshahallah!"

"Inshahallah!" Abbas was thrilled.

***

Abbas left him and headed back with a spring in his steps with a hope of becoming Jabbar Ellahi.

He would be the boss now. He ran with renewed energy and was impatient to share the good news with his trusted friends- Bilal, Changez, Kadar, Abrar.

***

Aditya met Javed and discussed the location.

"Shabbir Mallik lied to you. There wasn't anyone unwell there. It was not a doctor who visited that place," Javed informed, "Something is fishy there."

"Let's go and meet the man he met." Aditya told him.

"His name is Rehman, he owns a huge area, a cattle yard, many row houses, and slaughterhouses and is also known for arms trade." Javed knew them well.

***

Both Aditya and Javed reached Rehman's place. Rehman came out when he heard the vehicle. His face paled when saw Aditya and Javed together.

"Are you looking for something?" He asked.

"Why was Shabbir here?" Aditya asked directly.

"We know you work for Shabbir Mallik. This entire property actually belongs to Shabbir. You are just a care taker." Javed said calmly, "We need information about Jabbar Ellahi."

"No one would be spared if these 370 people get killed. No one." Aditya emphasized on 'no one' looking in to his eyes.

"Would you like to speak now?" Javed Khan was angry, "Or you want me to arrest you."

"I will definitely give you the information I have. Let me confirm it first. I don't want to give you half-baked stuff. Give me your phone number. I will call you myself and tell you when and where Jabbar will be available." Rehman spoke like a parrot.

They were happy that he spoke.

"I will make Jabbar available for you. But if you don't kill him, he will definitely kill all of us." Rehman was confident. Aditya was happy to get Jabbar's whereabouts.

"Don't worry. If he is here, he will not go back alive." Aditya assured him.

"When can we expect a call?" Javed wanted to plan his operation accordingly.

"Anytime tomorrow. Be ready." Rehman coughed and said.

Aditya and Javed left after sharing their cell numbers with him.

***

Aditya lit a cigarette and shared another with Javed.

They smoked and thought about Rehman. Everything looked too easy.

"Do you think Rehman will provide us right information? He agreed too easily."

"Yes. There must be something fishy. He knows where Jabbar is. He wants him dead. It might be a trap…" He didn't finish the sentence.

"It is possible that he is unhappy with Jabbar. Rehman knows everything, that is for sure. Jabbar and Rehman might have some major differences or fight…"

"We need to be extra cautious."

Aditya left to share the news with Jang Bahadur. He would require a backup for the operation.

***

Shabbir picked up the phone and looked out of the window at the darkness.

"There would be a deadly operation when Jabbar arrives here." Informed Rehman.

"Did they ask about me?" Shabbir asked.

"Yes, they asked why you came here? I told them someone was unwell. You came to see him. But he is fine now."

"Hmm." Shabbir was satisfied with the reply.

CHAPTER 20

Night broke into dawn.

Military was all set for an action-packed operation.

Lutyens's Delhi politicians were happy at the thought of Jabbar getting killed in the operation.

Iqbal hoped for another day of smooth shooting.

Jabbar wished Iqbal understood his passion for freedom. He did what Iqbal wanted, now it was his turn to reciprocate.

Shabbir Mallik called for Lukman who had just served him coffee. Now he was looking for his cigar. Lukman got his box. He smoked and relaxed. *Today was going to be a big day. Abbas would kill Jabbar and later he would kill all the hostages. He would be rewarded for that. The world would see that Kashmir situation is still deadly. Army couldn't save them. It would draw global attention.*

***

Ayesha was hopeful of a good coverage. She always wanted to be a famous journalist like Rajdeep, Karan, Barkha and Rajat. *Would she become one of them someday?* She was looking at Rahim. She had broken barriers and customs. She stayed with Rahim in the same hotel room.

Ayesha made tea, with the hot water from the electric kettle, tea bag and sugar. She looked at Rahim. He was sleeping like a baby. She went and sat in balcony attached to the room. She looked at the distant hills. Pune always drizzled. This was her first visit to Pune. She enjoyed the light cold. Srinagar's cold was bitter, the coolness of Pune soothed her.

Rahim opened his gunky eyes. He went to the washroom and looked into the mirror. He was in Pune for a story, with beautiful Ayesha. *Where was she? She wasn't in the room. Where had she gone?*

He got out of the washroom and saw Ayesha relaxing in the balcony. He joined her.

"Good morning!" Ayesha greeted him, "Did you sleep well?"

"I did. Thank you!"

Ayesha got up and made coffee for him. He thanked her silently with his smile. Ayesha's graceful face shone; breasts jiggled when she lifted both her hands to tie her long hair. Rahim's nerves rocked with sexual desire. He gulped the coffee to hide his feelings and brunt his tongue. Ayesha looked at him with a pleasant smile.

Both sat and silently enjoyed the view of distant hills.

***

Guddu, Babloo and Pankaj, the spot boys, were busy serving beverages to all the unit members.

Iqbal opened his eyes and saw Shweta trying to wake him up.

"You sleep like a log even in this situation."

"What situation?" Iqbal joked. He took the cup of coffee from Rafee.

"You know what situation!"

"We have to do the romantic song today." Chandni had selected the costumes.

He saw Crystal come out of the den.

Jabbar Ellahi was sipping coffee. She sat there. Rafee served her coffee too.

Shweta came and narrated the romantic song situation.

The song was played. Jabbar had to hug her, lift her in his arms and kiss her. Shweta briefed him like a professional and went.

Jabbar looked at Crystal. He hoped that she would object. She definitely wouldn't agree to a kiss, he thought. But she seemed okay with it.

Jabbar called Iqbal. Iqbal came immediately.

"What is this?" Jabbar asked him to come to his den, "Let's go in, we will talk about it."

They talked inside the den.

"Are you asking me to kiss her?" Jabbar objected.

"You have to hug her, lift her in your arm, roll with her on the grass and finally kiss her." Iqbal explained.

"Kiss her, just like that?"

"Kissing for the audience. Your story has to look real. You are kissing on the screen."

"But in front of everyone?"

"Yes," Iqbal just said casually, "It's just a kiss. That's it."

Jabbar looked nervous.

"Do you want a rehearsal first?" Asked Jabbar.

Iqbal was doubly confused. Rehearsal of a kiss meant he would kiss Crystal in the den and then in front of everyone.

"I can't kiss her." Jabbar refused.

"Okay. Have you gone to a hospital? Have you seen male doctors treat female patients? They see their patients semi-nude, sometimes even nude. Doctors focus on the disease and the treatment, not their body. It's a doctor's job! Kissing is your job as an actor. The hero is kissing the girl in the story. The audience should believe that you are in love with her. It has to look natural and candid."

Jabbar wasn't convinced. Iqbal decided to change the scene.

"No issue. I will make changes. The song will have everything hugging, lifting, rolling with each other but without the kiss – is that fine with you?"

"But would it look real?" Jabbar asked childishly.

What did this man want? Iqbal was bewildered.

"Iqbal let me do the rehearsal first," Jabbar suggested.

"Hmm." Iqbal went out and explained the situation to Crystal.

"It's up to you now. Your call." Iqbal kept chewing his nails. He was nervous about all that. He felt bad for Crystal.

"Don't chew your nails. I will handle it." Said Crystal and headed to the den.

Crystal smiled and entered the den.

"Hi!" she initiated, "You wanted to kiss me?"

"No. Who said that?" Jabbar didn't expect a direct question from her. He was zapped. "Did Iqbal say that? Call him now."

"No. He didn't. I guessed that," She smiled, "We have a romantic song to be shot this morning. Iqbal said the morning light is good for this kind of song."

"Yes." Jabbar was confused and quiet. He tried to defend himself like a schoolkid, "I actually told Iqbal to avoid it and do without a kiss sequence but…"

"But?" Crystal pretended that she is unaware of things.

"But he wasn't sure that will look real."

"So, what is the way out?"

"I don't know. You tell me!" Jabbar was irritated, "I hardly know anything about film making I am someone who knows how to pull a trigger and kill someone. I know how to blow a bomb."

"Do you want to kiss me Jabbar?" Crystal asked looking in to his eyes, before Jabbar could say anything she proposed, "Because I want to kiss you. I have never seen such a handsome guy in my life. I had fallen in love with you the moment I saw you." Crystal kissed him. Jabbar kissed her back. Crystal didn't give him a chance to think. It all happened in a moment.

The shooting began after an early breakfast.

Jabbar and Crystal's romantic scenes were very realistic. Their on- screen chemistry was magical.

Crystal was involved in delivering shots. She didn't know what prompted her to kiss a terrorist, a handsome terrorist. She actually fell in love with this guy when she saw him for the first time on the monitor. He was superb. She loved him when he touched her for the first time. She was a professional she never got involved easily. This was a unique situation. Jabbar had never touched a girl before– she figured. He wasn't interested in any of the girls except her. Love happened to her. She didn't know what would happen next. She went with the flow without thinking. That was the moment she loved a man who she didn't want to judge.

Bilal, Abbas, Kadar, Abrar and Changez were watching the shooting and seeing Jabbar kiss and romance a star. They were surprised at Jabbar. They were happy he had just a few more hours to live.

Bilal went to the cooking area where Rambabu- Shyambabu with spot boys were busy cooking.

"Do you need provisions?" Bilal asked, "Is it over?"

"We need it for dinner. We have just enough for lunch." Rambabu informed Bilal, "We told Mushtaq and Tipu. They have called someone to bring it."

"Hmm." Bilal said and walked to Abbas to inform him.

The shooting was interrupted because of sudden showers. Jabbar sat under the shed alone.

Salim and Tipu sat under another shed.

Abbas, Bilal, Changez, Kadar, Abrar ran and went behind the tempo. "There is no ration for dinner tonight." Bilal laughed and said, "Mushtaq had called Rehman to ask for rations. He has no idea he is calling his death."

"What did Rehman say?" He chuckled.

"Rehman must have assured him that it will be done."

"They will go mad when supplies don't reach post lunch."

* * *

Ayesha and Rahim dressed up and went to the lobby for breakfast. Rahim was wearing a full sleeved formal white shirt with navy-blue trousers. Ayesha had worn a red kurti paired with beige chinos.

"The complimentary buffet breakfast is served on the open terrace on the 7th floor." The receptionist informed them.

The open terrace was almost empty. They filled their plates and sat facing the hills.

"Can I ask you a personal question?" Ayesha was hesitant.

Rahim looked and waited for the question.

"Are you married?" Ayesha asked.

"No."

"Girlfriend?"

"Was in love once. She married someone else."

"Hmm," Ayesha continued the conversation "You have no girlfriend. Not married. Why the hell are you always lost? Is it Kashmir?"

"Yup. I feel betrayed. I always thought India was my country. I work in news agency which reports both the sides of the story. But the way Article 370 was revoked and everyone was locked down making Kashmir captive... It broke my trust. Where is the federal government? It's not just in Kashmir, there is no state working independently. The central government forces their decisions on state governments. It's like the CEO is running a company making centralized decisions. The center acts like a boss with all the state governments. The fabric of Buddha, Gandhi and Mahavir is missing. This is no more the same country. Politicians divert attention from the real issues. But what horrified me was the people of this country. Only a few raised their voice in support of Kashmir. Why?" Rahim let his grilled sandwich get cold, "One district magistrate from Kerala resigned in protest. That's it."

"It happened because people were hurt – Kashmir supported Pakistan. Pakistan made derogatory remarks time and again to hurt Indians. The rest of India was happy that Pakistan was taught a lesson." Ayesha contradicted.

Rahim pointed out, "Everything ends with Pakistan. Pakistan is a small country that is struggling to stand on its feet. How can India compare itself with Pakistan?"

"Terrorism was another factor attached to it, against which even Muslim nations didn't raise a voice." Ayesha added while eating idly with sambar.

Rahim was somber.

"My dad was killed. A stray bullet hit him. Mom got a heart attack soon after and passed away." Rahim took the coffee cup and said, "My little sister Nikhat went missing, she was never found. My brother Parvej left home and went to London never to return."

Ayesha knew there were many who were hurt in Kashmir just like him. "It is very complicated," Ayesha spoke in a low voice, "The other day an innocent man was killed by the terrorists because he opened his shop." Ayesha supported the government.

"Kashmir is very complicated to rule now." Rahim was animated. People around them turned to look at them. "People are killing people. They are misguided and angry." Rahim whispered when he realized he was drawing attention.

They got up and left. They had to cover many college students and send the interviews back to Rudra Shekhar.

CHAPTER 21

Jabbar looked puzzled. He had fallen in love with a girl.

Was that right?

He sat alone and looked at the lashing rain which had disrupted the shooting. He looked at the trees for a long time. *What was he doing?* He saw Mushtaq and Chandni chatting and laughing. Actually, the movie crew was not coming to his side. It was just the other way around. Iqbal had taken them to his side. He had become a *Bhand* now. He was ashamed of himself. *What did his men think when they saw him kissing, hugging, chasing and lifting Crystal?* This was all because of Iqbal. He instigated him.

Soon all of his men would become members of the film crew. They would be dancing on musical tunes soon. He was disappointed. Okay, he had given what Iqbal wanted. He didn't kill anyone. He didn't hurt anyone. He wanted him to act. Now it was Iqbal's turn. Iqbal should do the same from his side too.

He looked for Iqbal.

"Where is Iqbal?" He asked Rafee who was standing close to him awaiting any orders.

Rafee went in search of Iqbal. He was getting some shut eye in the vanity van.

"He is calling you," Rafee conveyed the message.

"Who?" Iqbal was drowsy.

"Boss, the big boss!"

Iqbal got the message.

"Can you please give me some black coffee?" He asked Rafee.

"Sure." Rafee ran to bring him coffee.

***

Iqbal went to Jabbar. He sat quietly as Jabbar looked serious. Jabbar had a joint ready for them to share. He lit his joint and passed it on to Iqbal.

"Do you know Iqbal how many of us sacrificed everything for Kashmir's freedom struggle?" Jabbar would indulge in a futile conversation again, Iqbal wasn't in a mood. He knew he would blow his brain now.

"The government's official data says 41,500 approximately." Iqbal had done his research during the script writing. He stubbed the cigarette butt after finishing it.

"Thousands have died just like that. Kids, young children, young men and women have fought against Indian government." Iqbal knew he was going to repeat the freedom issue again. He would never grow up. He looked for Rafee; where was he? He desperately needed black coffee to wake up. The cigarette helped a little but he needed coffee too. For him sleep was the most important relaxation, more than any drug. He wasn't getting enough sleep.

The rain was lashing.

He saw Rafee coming with a steaming coffee mug. He sipped hot coffee. Caffeine kicked into his brain. Nicotine and caffeine both helped him. He would be fine soon.

"I want you to talk to those who want to join the movement." Jabbar proposed randomly. Iqbal wasn't prepared for that. He wanted to complete the romantic song which was disrupted by the rain. He would get wonderful light after the rain. *How to deal with a man who was not ready to understand that it was all finished. Nothing could be done now. Kashmir was now a Union territory with assembly. Now everything was controlled by Delhi. This idiot wasn't ready to face the truth.* Iqbal was quiet. Jabbar repeated himself.

"Let me know who all are with us." Jabbar asked loudly.

"We are all with you Bhai," Iqbal replied.

"That's exactly my point … talk to them, tell them about it. After you finished talking to them. I will speak to them. Let's start the process."

Abbas, Bilal and Changez guessed something was wrong between Iqbal and Jabbar. They kept their eyes on them and tried to overhear from their shed.

Iqbal didn't know what to say. He sipped his black coffee.

"Do you know these are political games, just games … nothing but games!" Iqbal spoke fearlessly, "These are boundary line games. Pakistan, Bangladesh and India were one country. Now it's not. Did that make any difference in people's lives. Politicians are happy that 370 has been revoked in Kashmir and Pakistan has been humiliated. They divert our attention so that the real issues are evaded. They want controversies and issues so that people keep on fighting." He sighed and continued, "Do you know who are Honchos of these politicians? Arms making companies of the world. They decide who lives and who dies. They! They are so powerful that they can destroy the world in seconds if they unite and take a decision. These multinational companies do not have any country or religion. One country theory has vanished today. We live in an era where each country trades with other country. The politicians obey whatever these honchos say. They have money, they control the state. They help political parties and create issues so that countries fight and they sell their arms." Iqbal continued after a short pause.

"Where would they sell their arms if people don't fight? You know there is evidence to prove that F series making company supplied arms to both Iran and Iraq. The war continued for nine years. They need fighters and issues so that they can continue the war. They know they can win their seats in assembly and parliament just by keeping these issues alive." Iqbal sighed deeply.

Jabbar was listening quietly, so Iqbal continued, "Even if Kashmir gets freedom what would you have? Nothing... Few political families rule the nation as Congress ruled India for seventy years. You look handsome, you are talented why are you even thinking of going the other side of the fence. Politics is filth. Full of mud and dirt. You are a simple honest Kashmiri man. A performer. Everyone clapped when you performed. I bet you can't forget that in your entire life. Can you? Have you heard of Gandhi? He went to Africa, fought against British Colonialism. Did he take up arms? He didn't hurt anyone, didn't kill anyone and the entire world loved his approach. British had the most powerful army. He fought with a strategy and won."

Jabbar Ellahi interjected and said firmly, "I don't like Gandhi."

Iqbal replied immediately, "But he was a freedom fighter just like you." Iqbal paused to sip his black coffee.

"We don't follow him. He was a coward. Our purpose to free Kashmir." Jabbar was adamant.

"Bhai, freedom is a state of mind. You could be free even if your body is tied up in iron chains." Iqbal sipped coffee and continued,

"If you fight through nonviolence you would be known as freedom fighter. The moment you take up arms you become a terrorist. Game of freedom is the game of politicians. They use it to grab power. Innocent people fight in the name of freedom. Don't fall in the trap of political circus."

"How dare you to call it a circus?" Jabbar's firm voice cracked like a whip, "Have you forgotten. You said you will fight with me against Indian government. Your language has changed now. You try to tell me what is freedom? Gandhi? Nonviolence? Do you think you can fool me?" Iqbal was terrified when he looked at Jabbar's piercing eyes and angry red face.

Guddu and Rafee left them and stood in another shed. Shweta saw them and realized that something was amiss between Iqbal and Jabbar. The rain was at its peak. Iqbal decided to keep quiet.

"Have you forgotten who I am? I am the daddy of all honchos of the world."

"Bhai I am trying to explain what freedom is. The truth and nothing but truth." Iqbal's language provoked him more. He slapped him so tight that Iqbal was thrown out of the temporary tin shed.

Jabbar started kicking Iqbal with his gumboots. Abbas came running and said, "Allow me." Abbas had a club in his hand he started beating Iqbal with the club.

Jabbar saw that everyone was watching– tensed, holding their breath. He saw Crystal and the pained look on her face. He headed to the den. He entered the den and took out his weed packet, rolled a joint and lit it. He looked out through a small window and pulled a deep drag.

He suddenly sensed someone entering his den. He knew it must be Mushtaq so he continued looking out through the window.

"Kill that Bastard." Mushtaq said loudly, "Just tell me and I will shoot him." Jabbar knew Mushtaq for years. He meant not to kill Iqbal. He wanted to save Iqbal. He didn't like what Jabbar just did. But he had never gone against Jabbar's decision.

"Tell me please should I kill him right now?" Mushtaq said again, "Has he done something wrong? Tell me I will shoot him."

"Leave him." Jabbar said without looking at Mushtaq keeping his gaze out at the rain. Mushtaq left muttering 'leave him'.

He went out and instructed Abbas, "Stop. Stop. Leave him." Abbas turned towards Mushtaq and knew why he was instructing.

"What?" He didn't like Mushtaq shouting.

Mushtaq caught Iqbal's hand and lifted him.

"Bhai told me to stop. Means stop. Okay." Mushtaq looked in to Abbas's eyes. Abbas didn't reply. Iqbal was taken to vanity van for first-aid. His head was bleeding. His body was covered in bruises, blue, and black marks.

"Thank God. Mushtaq came on time." Shweta was very upset with Iqbal, "When everything was going well, why did you start a debate on Gandhi, freedom and nonviolence and all?"

Iqbal didn't say anything. Shweta and Mastani bandaged his head and hand.

CHAPTER 22

Crystal sat with Iqbal in the vanity van. Iqbal was assaulted badly.

He could have died today. Mushtaq saved him.

Jabbar couldn't stand to see Iqbal in this state. Iqbal was right; once you are friends, they wouldn't kill. No matter how deadly they were. They were very much interested in life. They liked them.

***

Jabbar sat alone for some time. What Iqbal said wasn't a lie. He had a point. The differentiation between a terrorist and a freedom fighter made sense.

The only person who benefitted from this violence was Shabbir and separatist leaders like him. He had robbed banks for him. Killed innocent people, bombed buses– for what? Shabbir Mallik ordered him. They manipulated us sitting in their cozy bungalows.

Iqbal was right; Shabbir had a lavish lifestyle. Jabbar knew people were using him in the name of patriotism. So typical of all politicians. Hitler used it and Germany faced war for many years. The entire world was forced to suffer because of him.

***

The Prime Minster was informed– today or latest by tomorrow Jabbar Ellahi would be killed.

Ajit Dayal was confident, "We are this close to them."

"What about the movie unit?" Asked the Home Minister.

"We have spread the net to trap Jabbar Ellahi. He will come out from his hole to meet someone. He will be either killed or caught," Dayal described his plan, "Dead or alive Jabbar Ellahi would be in our clutches. We have to wait and watch."

PM sighed– a long sigh of relief.

There was silence for a while. PM looked at Dayal who was eager to reply any questions.

The meeting went on for a few more minutes. Everyone was instructed to be prepared. They had to wait for the operation. Before that nothing could be done.

***

Rahim and Ayesha reported the views of college students about Kashmir, abducted movie crew and patriotism. Students spoke against Pakistan. Almost all thought that Pakistan should be attacked and finished. Enough was enough.

Rahim asked them quoting Samar Nakhate's interview, "Have you seen your teacher's reaction?"

"Yes, Nakhate Sir's video is viral on social media." One of them replied.

"But your reactions don't match with his thought process, he is talking not to avenge anyone, he has appealed even to the terrorist not to harm innocent film crew." Ayesha asked.

"We aren't saints like him or Gandhi. "Another girl replied and left.

They covered many colleges MIT, Symbiosis, Fergusson and Pune University.

They thought their job was done. But Shekhar wanted them to go to Mumbai and stay till the issue got resolved.

"Go back to Mumbai and try to cover movie stars." Shekhar encouraged them.

Both, Ayesha and Rahim headed for Mumbai.

CHAPTER 23

Lunch was ready to be served. Mushtaq was hungry. Entire atmosphere was tense. Guddu, Rafee, Babloo and Pankaj were waiting for orders. Mushtaq asked them to serve everyone.

Guddu and Rafee started organizing plates in front of Jabbar. He looked at the young boys silently.

"Where are you from?" Jabbar asked.

"I am from Mumbai, Saki Naka." Rafee said.

Jabbar looked at Guddu, "And you?"

"I am form Ghaziabad, UP. I work in Mumbai."

Jabbar looked at the innocent efficient young boys working day and night. They didn't know if they will go back alive, but they were happy serving everyone.

Then he saw Crystal at the entrance of the den.

"May I come in?" She smiled at Jabbar. Jabbar smiled. He knew she didn't like what had happened an hour earlier.

She came and sat. Guddu ran out for another plate.

"So?" Crystal smiled.

"So?" Jabbar smiled too.

"You didn't invite me for lunch?" Crystal complained.

"Look it was Iqbal who provoked me." Jabbar justified.

"Did I ask you anything?" Crystal looked in to his eyes, "I asked why you decided to …" she didn't complete the sentence.

"Decided to…" Jabbar wanted to know what was she up to.

"Decided to have lunch alone." Crystal completed her sentence. She was always happy. Jabbar realized.

"I was about to call you."

"Really?" Crystal was in mood to tease him. She knew he could not get irritated with her.

"Honestly speaking, I was scared of you." Jabbar said looking at the plate readied by Guddu and Rafee. They left after serving.

"You… scared of me?" Crystal laughed, "That is the biggest joke I have ever heard in my life."

Jabbar smiled. He looked at Crystal laughing heartily. He didn't know what to do. He took his plate and started eating. Crystal took hers too. She knew he had fallen in love with her. At the end of the day he was a man who had never touched a woman. She knew him now. The terrorist inside him was dying.

Jabbar and Crystal had a good time. They chatted and relished the lunch. Jabbar was back in a joyful mood. He saw Abbas and Mushtaq at the entrance.

He hinted them to come inside.

"There is no ration left." Mushtaq informed.

"Call Rehman." Jabbar said casually.

Mushtaq called Rehman who asked him to talk to Shabbir.

"Shabbir wanted to discuss some urgent matter with Jabbar." Rehman told Mushtaq. Mushtaq called Shabbir Bhai.

"You come down with Jabbar and bring someone from the film unit. Get that director Iqbal." Shabbir Mallik said and hung up.

"He is calling you. He wants to discuss something urgently which he doesn't want to talk over the phone." Mushtaq said and waited for Jabbar's reply.

"Why does he need me for ration?" Jabbar was skeptical.

Mushtaq called Mallik on the satellite phone again.

"It's not for food items Jabbar. I have to share some news with you. Plus, I haven't seen you for so long. Let's meet at Rehman's place this afternoon." Shabbir Mallik said convincingly.

"Okay." Jabbar hung up.

Jabbar knew provisions were needed.

He looked at Mushtaq.

"Shabbir Bhai has asked me to take Iqbal with us." Jabbar was worried.

"We will go with Iqbal." Jabbar concluded.

***

Iqbal rested in the vanity van for some time after lunch. He got up and heard that he had to go with Jabbar.

Shweta had a strong negative intuition when she saw Iqbal leaving with Jabbar and his men. Mushtaq assured her, "We are going to collect provisions. Everything is fine."

Shweta knew everyone felt insecure when Iqbal left. Iqbal was their strength. They trusted Iqbal. They had seen him facing difficulties and coming out of it.

CHAPTER 24

Shweta was from Delhi. Her parents didn't support her decision to join the creative world. She landed in Pune after much persuasion.

***

"What is this creative world?" Her Mom asked.

Dad looked at her as if she was going to rob a bank.

"Why?" Asked Dad.

"Why not?" Shweta replied.

"This is an uncertain industry. People struggle for years to get success. Few get, most of them don't make it, they fail." Dad reasoned why it was a bad choice for a career.

"Are you saying that people fail only in this industry?"

"No, but more in this industry. Also, girls are not safe."

"Girls are not safe anywhere in this country Dad. See the data. Any incident happens in the film industry is blown up as 'breaking news'. Because it's show business it always gets high exposure. Do you know a noble profession like education has many cases of girl abuse? Professors pressurize students to make compromises with them. Haven't you read it in the newspapers or watched on television? No one knows how many, because they don't even get reported." Shweta made her point.

"I will not work against your wish." Shweta said at the end of the conversation. She was fed up trying to make them understand. She gave up. She hardly participated in any conversation with her parents.

Shweta's Dad took a month. He discussed with his friends and relatives.

"She will not be happy if you force her. Let her face the music, she will regret her decision and come back. But if you go against her decision, she will never forgive you. She will always hold it against you." Her uncle advised her father, "These kids nowadays need to be handled with care. In our times, decisions were made by our parents, today they make their own decisions."

Shweta's dad had no option but to support her. She came to Pune, joined FTII and met Iqbal.

***

Iqbal was from Jaipur. Iqbal wasn't as lucky as Shweta.

He was star gazing on the terrace that night. He was sad, missing his Mom. They had a couple of pegs down. Iqbal opened up.

"My parents wanted me to be there, do something in Jaipur. We are three brothers. I am the middle one. My father never digested that I am making a career in films." He sounded very sad.

Iqbal was very hardworking, sincere and talented; but things didn't work for many years. He had started losing hope recently and then out of the blue *Azadi* came his way.

Shweta knew he was the best.

He tamed down a terrorist. He had great 'people' skills and solid research. He was different. He took risks and saved all of us. But today when he was leaving with Jabbar she was very apprehensive.

CHAPTER 25

Iqbal had no idea where he was going. He had bandages on his head and arm, he was aching all over. Jabbar was driving. Iqbal was sitting beside him. Tahir, Waqar and Imran were standing with their AK47s looking around. Any attacker would be killed instantly.

Maqsood, Mansoor, Afroz, Tipu & Salim were standing at the back of the jeep with their AK47s, dead alert.

Mushtaq and Omar were riding their bikes in front of Jabbar's Jeep.

"Where are we headed?" Iqbal broke the silence.

"We are meeting a friend and collecting groceries."

Jabbar said patiently. He looked normal and calm.

***

"Call everyone and make them sit here on the ground." Abbas ordered. Ghulam Hasan didn't like taking orders from Abbas. Ghulam was guarding the edge of the plateau.

"Who has asked you to do it?" Ghulam Hasan asked.

"Abbas is the boss when Jabbar and Mushtaq are absent." Bilal replied. Ghulam smelt a rat.

Abbas ordered everyone to sit in a circle again. Bilal and Kadar repeated Abbas's order. Crystal, Shweta, Mastani, Mallika and Chandni requested everyone to follow Abbas's instructions as they knew Abbas would kill if his orders were not followed.

Abbas knew he had to wait for some time– till Jabbar reached Rehman's place.

There was a pin drop silence amongst the film crew. No one spoke. They felt danger looming large. Fear gripped their hearts.

Changez was tall and deadly looking. He looked at the girls with hungry eyes. They were very scared. Crystal sensed some serious problem with Abbas's intention.

Everyone realized that they were dealing with Abbas and his friends and not with Jabbar. Abbas and Changez had collected the arms, created a fence and cordoned them off in a tight circle.

They kept a watchful eye on them.

***

Jabbar's jeep stopped. Mushtaq and Omar stopped their bikes and removed the wooden 'rock'. Iqbal recalled Mushtaq talking about these rocks.

The jeep stopped again after about ten kilometers.

Mushtaq and Omar's bikes continued ahead and vanished in the thick of the jungle soon.

Jabbar heard a unique sound which was a green signal to move ahead. He started the jeep and drove slowly on the road. They had reached close to Rehman's place. The jeep stopped again. Mushtaq and Omar gave a green signal.

Jabbar moved his jeep slowly.

Rehman coughed.

Aditya Raghuvanshi and Javed Khan had taken positions on two sides. The moment Rehman coughed they were alerted. They sent signals to the police force and army to cordon off the area.

Rehman coughed twice again.

Why he was coughing so much? Mushtaq smelt a rat.

Mushtaq saw Rehman looking around. He signaled Tahir who jumped from the jeep and climbed onto a tree close by. Tahir showed his thumb down which meant danger. Maqsood, Mansoor, Afroz stood on the jeep with Tipu, Waqar and Imran. Six of them ready for the worst. Their fingers were ready to pull the trigger.

Mushtaq whistled and signaled danger. He whistled again which meant 'move back immediately'.

He turned the bike and hinted Jabbar to take a U turn.

"No one will shoot." Jabbar commanded.

He wanted to leave the place without any violence. He would deal with the traitor later. His prime intention was to quit the place.

Tahir started climbing down from the tree to get back to the jeep. Tipu, Waqar, Imran were ready to retaliate. They looked around and saw few bayonets facing them. They waited for Jabbar's order. Jabbar was taking a U turn.

Everyone heard a gunshot. Jabbar saw Tahir's dead body drop right in front of the jeep.

"Shoot." Jabbar ordered.

Aditya saw Jabbar's jeep. Six men Tipu, Waqar Maqsood, Mansoor, Afroz, and Imran started firing incessantly.

Javed & Aditya were in position and were shooting carefully taking aim. His team was spread strategically covering the back as well. They shot four of those standing in Jabbar's jeep. They had no idea that man in the driver's seat was Jabbar.

Both the sides exchanged fire.

Jabbar knew he had limited ammunition. He sped the jeep, but the jeep lost its balance as Tahir's dead body was lying right in front. The jeep went in to the ditch. Mushtaq, Omar and Salim started firing continuously, giving cover to Jabbar till he pulled the jeep from the ditch.

Aditya looked at Rehman and asked, "Who is Jabbar Ellahi?"

Rehman hinted at the jeep. Aditya couldn't figure out as Mushtaq, Salim, Omar were covering the jeep. Iqbal was observing everything.

Jabbar tried to take his jeep out from the ditch. Mushtaq shot Rehman and his two men when he saw him communicate with Aditya.

Omar took out few a smoke shells and threw them. These bombs created a lot of smoke. Aditya and his team couldn't see anything.

Aditya and Javed were trying to figure out who and where Jabbar was.

Iqbal jumped from the right to the left side and took the driver's seat, pushing Jabbar. He covered Jabbar. Aditya stepped ahead and risked his life. He wanted to kill everyone except Iqbal. He knew Jabbar was one of them. There was smoke and vision wasn't clear. He fired at the people inside the jeep. In the meantime, Iqbal jolted the jeep pressing hard on clutch and accelerator. The jeep jumped out from the pit. Iqbal drove the jeep with full speed.

Aditya took a chance and pulled the trigger again. Iqbal moved his hand and pulled Jabbar down. As an upshot the bullet scratched Iqbal's arm. It started bleeding.

Mushtaq and Omar started their bikes and followed the jeep. Moments later smoke was cleared.

Aditya saw Rehman's dead body. Rehman's two men were down too. Five bloody bodies were spread on the jungle dirt road.

Javed came to him. "Any casualty?"

"Not from our side." Aditya replied.

Aditya called the General.

"Five of them are down from their side, no casualty from our side. Our informer Rehman and his men got shot." Aditya paused and continued "Total eight people have been shot."

"Jabbar?" General asked.

"I have no idea. Jabbar could be one of the dead." Aditya explained, "Rehman knew him. He is dead now. Few fled by a jeep. We need helicopters to find them. I know the direction they took."

"Okay." General Jang Bahadur was brief.

He called Ajit Dayal. Ajit carried the news further up and said. "Chase those rats. I am sending helicopters." Ajit Dayal asked for quick action, "Before they kill any of the movie crew members kill them all."

***

Iqbal drove the jeep in full speed. Iqbal's arm was bleeding.

"I will drive." Jabbar said. Iqbal stopped the jeep for a moment and let Jabbar take over.

The bullet had brushed Iqbal's arm. Jabbar looked at him proudly and gratefully. Iqbal had saved his life and taken a bullet for him too. He could have died.

"You saved my life." Jabbar was thankful. Iqbal smiled.

"If you die, my movie would be incomplete. You are my hero now." Iqbal smiled, "You are in continuity, I can't cast someone else."

"For you, everything is the movie?"

"Yes. For me everything is movie. My life is my movies. I can die for it. I can't think beyond my films." Iqbal was serious, "Day and night, morning, evening– I eat, drink and dream movies."

"You can't be serious." Jabbar asked.

"I am." Iqbal replied. They heard the bikes.

Mushtaq was on one bike. Salim and Omar were on the other.

Jabbar recalled the entire incident. Shabbir had called to kill him. He hatched the conspiracy.

Jabbar's five men were killed.

***

Abbas was sure that Iqbal and his team would have gone to Allah by now. Time to announce his name as Jabbar Ellahi.

"I am Jabbar Ellahi." Abbas proclaimed in front of everyone, "Jabbar Ellahi was killed. I am the new Jabbar Ellahi."

"The rules have changed now. We will kill and send a few cadavers today." Bilal announced loudly.

"We will start with the girls." Abbas paced and talked, "We have to complete the task the ex-Jabbar Ellahi was supposed to finish. We have to send bodies to government of India." Abbas lit a bidi.

Kadar caught Crystal's hand.

Chandni, Mastani and Mallika were scared.

"Do you know my name film star?" Kadar chuckled and said, "I am Kadar, but not that actor Kadar Khan. I am Kadar Bhasin."

Abbas stepped ahead smiled and took Crystal's hand from Kadar's clutch.

Abbas said looking at everyone present there in his loud voice, "You flirted with ex Jabbar Ellahi. The new Jabbar will rape you in front of everyone. We will make a video of that rape and send to every mobile to watch." Abbas reached out for his belt.

Kadar came with another advice, "Let's take these four girls at a time. It will be exciting."

Abbas said, "Not a bad idea."

Kadar, Bilal, Changez moved ahead, caught Chandni, Mastani and Mallika's hand. They started hugging, kissing & touching their bodies. Girls struggled to get rid of him.

Abrar took a cell phone and started filming.

***

Jabbar Ellahi was speeding his jeep to reach his hide-out as soon as possible.

Mushtaq was speeding on his bike.

They knew Shabbir Mallik wanted Jabbar dead. Jabbar recalled all those times when Shabbir used him for atrocities.

"You are my trusted kid. No one can touch you." Shabbir always sweet talked him in to confidence, "There is a big consignment coming from Afghanistan."

Jabbar and his men smuggled the arms and ammunition from Afghanistan. Later, Jabbar and his men robbed a bank and blew a military truck because Shabbir Mallik wanted him to.

He killed innocent people because Shabbir Mallik wanted it. Today five of his men were down because Shabbir betrayed him and wanted him dead. Shabbir was a monster who killed people. He obeyed a monster's orders in the name of freedom. At the end of the day what did he get? A tag of terrorist. He didn't want to be Shabbir Mallik's dog, not anymore.

History will remember him as a terrorist; not as a freedom fighter.

Iqbal was right. It's a power game. He & his friends were used. Arm making companies want to sell their guns, missiles, bombs and rocket launchers. They need people and issues so that they kept on fighting and bought their products. It was business at the end of the day and politicians and arm dealers made money. People like him were being used.

***

A flight of helicopters were ready for the operation.

This government was quick on decision. Especially when there was an enemy to fight.

The helicopters took off in the direction terrorist had vanished.

They were prepared for the worst. The backup was ready if Pakistan attacked. The entire army was on red alert.

"It's border area." General discussed with the defense minister.

"Go ahead even if you have to go inside Pakistan and kill them you have a 'go ahead'. Do not hesitate. We are ready for the war if need be." The defense minister was rock steady. Pakistan needed to be taught a lesson. Unless he was tough, people of the country wouldn't vote for him. The people of India wanted tough stand against Pakistan. People forgot anything and everything else till Pakistan issue was kept alive.

This not just India's story. It was a global story. In USA, Trump was elected who was known to be decisive and action oriented. He ordered a huge boundary wall between Mexico and USA. In the United Kingdom, Brexit happened. In France, Yellow West Protest started against the government. The PM was aware of the blowing wind of the world. He didn't want to go against the storm. He always went with the flow and in fact, used it to his advantage.

***

Crystal and Chandni exchanged looks. They decided to fight back. There was no sign of Iqbal, Jabbar and the terrorists who were friendly. Abbas and his friends wanted to kill them eventually. They decided to fight and die.

Crystal bit Abbas's hand and ran. Chandni too ran away behind Crystal. Abbas and Bilal ran behind them. Mastani and Mallika watched as they had no chance to escape.

Everyone heard a gunshot. Abbas fell down on the ground with a thud. The bullet hit him in the chest. His eyes were still open.

He saw Jabbar Ellahi was alive standing with Mushtaq, Tipu, Iqbal and Salim.

Kadar, Changez, Bilal and Abrar were shocked to see Jabbar alive. *How did he survive? He was supposed to be dead.*

Crystal rushed and hugged Jabbar. She cried like a baby. Kadar, Bilal and Changez froze.

Abrar stood stunned.

They couldn't believe Jabbar Ellahi was back. He was standing right in front of them like an undead ghost.

"Didn't I warn you?" Jabbar asked.

"Forgive me please. It was Shabbir Mallik who instigated us." Abbas said in a low voice, "He said I would be made Jabbar Ellahi." He knew he would die soon, "I am sorry I believed him Bhai."

"You feel sorry. You know five of our friends have died and you feel sorry? And you listened to Shabbir Mallik and betrayed me." Jabbar was angry.

"Traitors." Mushtaq said angrily "Our friends died because of these traitors. They don't deserve to be alive." Mushtaq was livid.

Jabbar looked at Mushtaq. He understood Jabbar's hint.

Kadar, Bilal, Abrar, Abbas and Changez were killed instantly. Mushtaq and Omar shot them all.

"Abbas wanted to become Jabbar Ellahi. He has been made Jabbar Ellahi. Anyone else wants to become Jabbar Ellahi?" Mushtaq yelled.

Crystal was trembling. She felt the difference between fiction and reality. It was deadly. She experienced a near rape and near death. She was shattered.

They heard a helicopter overhead.

"Army has started their operation." Mushtaq looked up.

"Jabbar Ellahi has been killed." Iqbal cocked his head and looked at Jabbar, "You are my artist- Azad. My Hero. Allah has given you a chance. Let's leave for Mumbai." Iqbal offered.

Jabbar was stunned.

Everyone gathered and stood in front of Iqbal, Jabbar and Mushtaq.

"Bury your guns. Time to bite the bullet." Iqbal announced loudly. Everyone looked at Iqbal whose head was bandaged, one hand was hung with bandage strip and another arm was bleeding profusely. He roared like a tiger.

Tears rolled down Jabbar's cheek. Iqbal was trustworthy. He was a great guy.

"Terrorists are dead," Iqbal pointed at the bloody bodies of Abbas, Changez, Kadar, Abrar and Bilal. He looked at Jabbar again, "What are you thinking?"

"You are our Azad now." Iqbal looked at Jabbar and scanned everyone else, "Everyone who is here belongs to movie industry. Understand?"

"Yup." Mushtaq yelled cheerfully.

"Any questions? Anyone?" Iqbal asked, "They fed us. They saved us. Now they would be part of us. If anyone has problems this is the time… tell me now. Otherwise forever keep quiet." Iqbal urged the crew members to accept them.

"There is no 'they'. It only 'us." Kabir said.

"Yes, it's us. We all belong to Bollywood."

"I am Azad. Let's leave." Azad said loudly.

Iqbal got on to a big rock so that he can address everyone. He almost shouted, "Are we good to go as one team?"

"Yes!" Everyone shouted in unison.

"Welcome to the club." Iqbal shook hands with Azad and hugged him. Crystal was the next to hug him. Too much had happened in a few minutes but there was no time to mull over it.

Mushtaq yelled, "Take the buses and trucks, SUVs, all vehicles; we are leaving now. Hurry up! Make it fast." Everyone jumped from their place like a spring.

They hopped in the vehicles and took off hastily.

***

Aditya used binoculars and found a few platforms at the tree tops. There were temporary tin sheds in four corners. It was a plateau surrounded by a huge trench. They lowered the helicopters. They noticed the dead bodies and also signs of habitation. They decided to land the choppers there.

"This could be a trap. The dead bodies could be decoy, be careful." Aditya said and decided not to land at all but hang the choppers midair. They came down using ropes and stepped ahead slowly and carefully.

They saw corpses of five terrorists–Abbas, Changez, Kadar, Abrar and Bilal.

"Only five terrorists?" Aditya was surprised and so was Javed.

"Five were killed at Rehman's place." Javed added the number, "Ten in total."

"Ten people abducted 370 people?" Aditya wondered.

"Where are the hostages?" Javed was concerned about the film crew. "Where was Iqbal and the movie unit? Are they safe? And if they abducted the entire film unit, who killed them? Or were they moved?" No one had any answer to Javed's queries.

"Who is Jabbar? Is he among the dead?" Javed murmured.

Each and every one who was present there, had questions.

No one had any answers.

A fleet of vehicles drove down the hill.

***

Shabbir Mallik had no idea what happened that day. No clue at all. He was restless and smoking one cigar after another.

Rehman and his men were not in communication.

Abbas was not picking up the satellite phone. Was Jabbar killed? Or was Abbas killed? Or all of them were killed? Was it an army operation? But what happened in that operation? Who survived, who didn't?

He looked in the darkness and decided to wait and watch.

***

The speeding vehicles were stopped at a military check post when they hit the main road.

The vehicles stood in a row. The army officer got into bus with his associates. Iqbal, Azad chose to sit with Mushtaq and others in the bus. Crystal, Chandni, Mastani, Mallika, were in the SUV.

"Hello." Iqbal smiled.

"Hello there. You are hurt, your arm is bleeding." The army officer saw Iqbal's condition, "Get him first-aid." he instructed the solider standing behind him. Azad was watching them holding his breath. He looked at Mushtaq who was all alert and ready for action.

The officer stepped ahead, stopped suddenly and turned back and stood close to Iqbal, "You are Iqbal, right?" He recognized Iqbal.

"Yes I am." Iqbal smiled.

He shook hands with Iqbal, "Everyone was talking about you. So, what happened there? Everyone okay? Did anyone…?"

Iqbal understood what he meant, "No one from our team died fortunately, we are safe. We are free now. We are good to go. All the terrorists are dead. Please inform everyone, we don't have our mobile phones." Iqbal was brief.

The solider came with the first aid kit. Started cleaning Iqbal's blood off his arm. Iqbal's shirt was soaked in blood. Iqbal stood behind driver's seat while the solider gave him first-aid.

"I have seen you somewhere? Do I know you?" He looked at Azad and asked.

"He is the hero of my film *Azadi*." Iqbal replied promptly.

"What's his name?"

"Azad." Iqbal replied as Azad was silent.

"Why is he not talking?"

"Shocked. He is shocked. We all were abducted for over two days." Iqbal explained and asked, "Have you heard of Jabbar Ellahi?"

"He is a dreaded terrorist."

"Have you seen him?" Iqbal asked again.

"Yes. I think I have seen him." His reply shocked Iqbal and others.

Azad was silent. Mushtaq's hand went to his revolver.

The army officer put his hand in the pockets of his pants.

Mushtaq was ready to spring in to action. Iqbal didn't know what to do. He waited as the soldier kept him busy.

"The bullet has just touched your arm. You are lucky." The solider said after checking his wound and cleaning it with Savlon and bandaging it off. He gave Iqbal a few tablets, "Take it now. Just pain killers." He gave Iqbal a water bottle. Iqbal realized he was thirsty; he took one tablet with an entire bottle of water.

Tension built as army officer took his hand out of his pocket. Mushtaq was ready to shoot if he took his revolver out. Omar was also alert. The army officer took out his cell phone and asked, "Can I please take a selfie with you?"

"Sure, why not." Before Azad said anything, Iqbal replied immediately.

Azad smiled. Mushtaq was relieved.

Army officer on duty took a selfie with Azad. He got off the bus with his colleague.

"Be prepared, people will take selfies with you," Iqbal smiled. Azad heard him and looked out through the window– the fresh air hit his face.

Azad sighed. He felt good. He would be in Mumbai. The city he had heard a lot about. Never in his wildest dreams he had imagined himself going there to become an actor. It was Allah's wish.

All vehicles headed to the airport.

Iqbal looked at Mushtaq and called him close. Mushtaq came close and bent to hear Iqbal, "Are you carrying a gun? You know there would be a thorough check before you board the plane." Iqbal whispered.

"I know, don't worry." Mushtaq said.

***

Aditya and Javed got the information that Iqbal and the entire movie crew was safe and sound. The message was conveyed to PMO and later to the media.

Sampit was the man who addressed media in Delhi.

"I have good news to share with you. The army planned a very successful operation against the terrorists. All terrorists were shot dead. Let me emphasize - 'No casualties on our side. Everyone is safe'. The investigations are on. Prima facie, it seems the terrorists were from Pakistan. Trained and sent to escalate the Kashmir issue." He concluded with a cheerful smile, "Our prime minister and home minister didn't sleep and kept guiding us. A plan was executed thereafter."

"When are they reaching Mumbai?" Asked a reporter.

"Soon." He informed.

"Our government is serious about tackling terrorists. We had information about Jabbar Ellahi and his men. We don't take nonsense, we act."

The media conference ended with it.

The government congratulated the army and took full credit.

CHAPTER 26

Sheikh Ul-Alam International Airport, Srinagar.

"I will be back in a couple of hours. Wait for me. There is one assignment to be finished." Azad said. Iqbal smiled. He knew where Azad was headed. Azad and Mushtaq headed out of the airport with Omar and Salim

***

The chief of airport authority Anwar Bani personally attended to the crew members and served snacks, dry fruit packets and beverages immediately. He saw Crystal and smiled.

"I am a big fan of yours." the forty-five-year-old man grinned. Crystal smiled in response. He recognized Iqbal too, "I have seen you on TV. You look different from your picture."

"I am sure I do!" Iqbal just smiled.

Iqbal had to count everyone to convey to authorities so that the numbers matched. He asked Kabir to check if everyone reached. He came out with a number which worried Iqbal.

"They are thirty-one. We are 370 so the total comes to four hundred one." Kabir was worried.

"A team of doctors is going to visit you soon." Anwar Bani had called authorities as he was worried about Iqbal's condition.

Everyone stared at Iqbal and Crystal when they arrived. For Crystal, it was normal as she was a huge star. Iqbal enjoyed the attention for the first time.

He realized that he too was famous now. Everyone at the airport was looking at him because he was in the news. It was a good feeling to be in spot light before his first movie was even made.

"You are famous now." Shweta smiled and hugged him, "See everyone is looking at you."

Iqbal's attention was somewhere else. He knew there were many challenges ahead. The extra thirty-one men will have to be explained to people who knew the exact number- 370.

"Tell everyone not to discuss anything about Azad." Iqbal delegated the task to Shweta.

Dr. Asif Kazi looked at Iqbal. "Take this medicine," He advised, "You need to rest. Take this when you board the plane. This will make you sleep for a few hours. You will feel drowsy when you reach Mumbai Airport." Dr. Asif Kazi told him warmly, "We are proud of you Iqbal."

Iqbal smiled back.

"Thank you, Doctor." Iqbal shook his hand.

***

Azad, Omar Salim and Mushtaq hopped into a cab.

"Where to?" the taxi driver asked.

"Drive, I will guide you." Mushtaq handed him a few two thousand rupees notes, "Keep it. You are booked for a round trip."

"Till the morning Sir?"

"No, just a few hours. We will be back soon." Azad assured him.

They needed the vehicle to return.

***

Shabbir watched the news with Muneer Lone. He had hardly any clue. His brain was stormed with a series of thoughts. The television was constantly 'breaking news'.

"Terrorists killed ... movie unit is safe... going back to Mumbai soon."

Where was Jabbar Ellahi? No one confirmed if he had been killed. The terrorist pictures were made available to the media.

Aditya Raghuvanshi and Javed Khan along with Ajit Dayal handled queries from the journalists.

"Hostage crisis is over. I congratulate our brave soldiers for a successful operation." Ajit Dayal said and moved.

"Who killed them?" asked one of the journalists.

"I just replied, our brave soldiers ..." He left after that short reply.

Shabbir Mallik heard a gunshot. He got up and looked out of the window. His man Friday Liyakat was dead outside the bungalow. He saw four people entering his living area.

Before Shabbir said anything, Mushtaq shot Muneer Lone who tried to escape. His dead body was sprawled on the ground. The white marble floor turned red. Luckman came from the kitchen, saw Azad, Omar, Salim and Mushtaq. He ran back. Mushtaq shot him too.

"Kid, you are my child, like my son. I made you Jabbar– Jabbar Ellahi." Shabbir pretended to be happy to see him though his face was ashen with fear.

"I am here to thank you." Azad said with all seriousness. "I know what you did and what you do." Azad said, "You informed the army and police to finish Jabbar Ellahi. Jabbar Ellahi is dead, I am Azad, a free man."

"Please sit. I can explain what happened. The traitor was Abbas and Rehman. You have been misinformed."

"Explain." Azad gave him one last chance. Azad walked to the kitchen, took a water bottle and sipped on slowly.

Shabbir didn't know what to say. He had no idea whether Abbas was alive or dead. *Did Abbas tell him about the trap?* His mouth went dry.

"Time up." Mushtaq said, "You have nothing to say."

"Adios." Azad said.

Azad shot him. He didn't waste any time. Mushtaq, Salim, Omar and Azad hopped back in the same cab parked at a little distance and left for the airport.

***

Aditya Raghuvanshi, Ajit Dayal and Javed Khan reached the airport. They met Iqbal.

"Have you taken any medicine?" Ajit asked him sympathetically.

"Yes. Soldiers at the check post gave me first-aid." Iqbal was humble and obliged, "I am really thankful to everyone."

"Hmm." Ajit smiled and asked another question, "So how did it all happen? How many were they? What was their plan?"

"They were many. They came and left in shifts. There was an old person called Rehman who was providing them ration and other stuff." Iqbal cooked up a story, "He was one of them."

"So, do you think Rehman was Jabbar Ellahi?" Question came from Javed Khan. He thought something was amiss.

Iqbal was quiet. He didn't know what to say.

"No idea. Rehman spoke like he was the boss."

"Do you know who Jabbar Ellahi was?" Ajit Asked a question which made Iqbal conscious, "You might have seen him. Can you recognize his body? I have their photographs with me." Ajit took his cell phone to show the pictures of the dead men found at the crime scene.

"What I gathered in past two days is - no one was Jabbar Ellahi." Iqbal replied calmly, "They use to take instructions from satellite phone calls. Every day, a new person was the leader – Jabbar Ellahi." Iqbal explained, "There was always a fight for being the leader." Iqbal informed, "They fought and killed each other."

"Why had they gone down to Rehman's place?" Aditya asked.

"Provisions were over." Iqbal had a quick reply "Today Rehman didn't come, he called them to collect the supplies."

"But what did they discuss exactly?" Question came from Javed Khan. Ajit was listening quietly, focusing on Iqbal's replies.

"All the discussions were held inside a den. Two of them rushed out suddenly, yelling and took out their guns. We heard the firing from the den. One terrorist had been shot. Before we could understand anything there was exchange of fire. They killed each other." Iqbal sighed, "Without a second's delay, we decided to run for freedom, without looking back."

"They were only five of them – they made you all hostages?" Ajit.

He tried to tie up the loose ends.

They were many. Today they had some plan which failed. They took me with them. They were as many as fifteen of them."

"Five were killed." Aditya interjected, one was Rehman and two of his men. If Rehman was their leader– then total terrorist killed were five plus three, that's eight.

Rehman and his two men were not with them; they were Shabbir's men. Javed calculated, "Five near Rehman's place and five at the hide out – so total ten men. What do you think?"

"I am not in a frame of mind to think straight right now. God saved us. There were lots of them but their fight for leadership saved us," he sighed. "Yes. The second group of almost twenty-five moved in another direction," Iqbal cooked a new story, "They were supposed to get back late in the night. But then this operation happened– thanks to you all." He knew these numbers were not enough to justify. Only ten terrorists taking 370 people hostages– it was not convincing at all.

"Hmm," Ajit was thinking hard, "So Jabbar Ellahi can come back again." Ajit was skeptical. He knew the problem wasn't over.

"Possible. It's a brand. Anyone who fought for Kashmir's freedom would brand himself as Jabbar Ellahi." Javed Agreed, "That is their new plan to keep it hot."

"No one has seen Jabbar Ellahi because there wasn't a guy called Jabbar Ellahi." Iqbal added.

That was news for them.

The snacks were served to the crew while they were talking to Ajit Dayal, Aditya and Javed.

"Can we leave for Mumbai?" Iqbal changed the topic.

"We have arranged a special plane for Mumbai. I have also asked for inflight catering. Do not worry. A doctor would accompany you till Mumbai. I am happy that everyone is going back safe– without a single casualty." Ajit was happy.

"So how many are you in total, 370. Right? We need to arrange a big Boeing so you can all go together." Asked Aditya.

"We are 401." Iqbal knew there was no record to prove the number as they all arrived on different dates, by different routes and modes.

"Jabbar Ellahi's video said it was 370."

"Big lie. He just wanted to use that number 370. It is far more fetching to say 370 for 370. It was a gimmick. It was all planned to get publicity globally. Also, they never really counted us." Iqbal was a writer, expert in cooking up stories.

"Hmm." He seemed convinced.

Ajit, Aditya and Javed shook hands with Iqbal and left.

Iqbal noticed Ajit Dayal was an intelligent, serious person. He was focused and didn't pay attention to anything other than questioning. He was sharp and looking for a clue to get something of use. He hardly noticed Crystal or anyone else. He didn't bother to talk to such a big star. Iqbal knew he was very close to the PM. He had played a big role in revoking Article 370. Now he was working to reinstate peace and normalize the situation in Kashmir.

***

Shekhar called Rahim and assigned him Iqbal's interview.

"Tonight, they will reach Mumbai. Make sure you talk to Iqbal or Crystal." Shekhar was excited about the story, "Take a video if possible, otherwise at least photos."

***

Azad and Mushtaq entered the airport. They saw everyone was busy hogging. They were starving too. Azad was quiet. He sat with his men for a while.

"How are you all? We have got a fresh start."

"You were our Bhai, now you are our hero. We will follow your orders in future as we did in the past. We left when you asked us to leave. Just one request Bhai. We will be together in this," Omar was emotional.

"We were together and we will be together. Don't worry."

Jabbar assured them and went to the loo. He couldn't recognize the person looking back at him from the mirror. He smiled looking at his image. He noticed a girl staring at him on his way out. He was embarrassed. She smiled at him. Azad smiled too.

"I am Saira." She said. Crystal looked at them. Crystal knew Azad was handsome and would draw female attention. She felt jealous.

She walked up to him. "Hi! Where did you go? Who is she?"

"I am Saira." Saira introduced herself. I am from Kashmir. I live in Mumbai. I am an actress too. Have you seen *Nagin*?"

"No," Crystal was rude, "I asked you where you went Azad?" Crystal looked in to Azad's eyes.

"Nowhere." He replied coolly. Saira left them talking.

He was Azad– he realized. Unbelievable, life was taking a drastic turn. Was that possible?

"Snacks? I am hungry" Azad sounded like a kid.

"Me too– very hungry!" Crystal smiled. Iqbal heard them.

Kabir arranged for snacks immediately. They enjoyed the sandwiches and soft drinks. Iqbal and Shweta came to him.

"We are good to go." Mushtaq added, "Your hero is ready to rock." Omar and Salim laughed.

"Where have you been blue eyed boy?" Crystal was not giving up.

"I had to meet an old friend and settle a very old issue." Azad smiled and said.

"I missed you." Crystal didn't prod further.

"Oh, really? I missed you too."

Mushtaq, Iqbal, Shweta watched them both blush.

"Where will we stay in Mumbai?" Mushtaq asked to change the topic. He found everyone staring at Azad and Crystal.

Iqbal replied biting his nails, "We will manage, once we reach Mumbai. Kabir will help us."

"Don't worry." Crystal came to the rescue, "I have an empty flat in Goregaon."

***

The doctor on the plane gave Iqbal a sleeping pill.

Iqbal took the pill and slept for three long hours. He had nightmares. He was chased by a pride of lions and he outran them to escape. He dreamt that Shweta, Crystal, Kabir, Mastani, Mallika, Guddu, Rambabu, Shyambabu ... all fell in the trench and kept falling down. He was pulled by Azad suddenly. He fought with some lions. Mushtaq smiled and said – Bhai saved you again. The nightmare continued – Kashmir leaders, politicians, stone pelting kids on the roads of Kashmir– stone throwers ran – army chased them down...

Jabbar and Mushtaq had more cold drinks.

"What if ..." Mushtaq tried to say something.

Azad interjected, "We have seen what Allah had planned for us." He looked out at the clouds. Fluffy, white clouds indicated that everything was going to be fine.

"Ammi wanted me to become a hero." Azad got sentimental, "A director from Mumbai came and made me a hero. We had no choice then when we were killers and have no choice now."

***

Rahim reached the airport around 11:00 PM with Ayesha.

Special investigation on stories by the media had become a joke as there were no free media in this country. Everyone was joking in the name of journalism.

Reporters worked like employees. They took fat salaries, obeyed orders, drank free liquor, went home– and the next day, the same routine. Rahim wasn't okay with it. He had applied for a job in a big news agency. He was a bit disappointed as he got no positive response.

He looked at Ayesha. This cute Kashmiri girl was trying her luck in the big bad world of media. They sat in a lavish café. They had no idea how long they will have to wait–it seemed endless.

"Wait there. I am in touch with the authorities. I will call you once the plane lands." Shekhar had his network.

"Do you like this job?" Ayesha asked him out of the blue.

"I hardly have any choice," Rahim sounded like a loser, "What about you?"

"I want to do something for Kashmir." Ayesha was passionate.

"If you really want to do something for Kashmir, leave reporting." Rahim was harsh, he always underestimated her. She looked at him. *He is a man. He thinks like a man– always judging her capabilities as a professional and undermining her.*

Rahim was often blunt and rude. Ayesha didn't like his reply.

He was different from others. Something about him was magnetic that kept wanting her to be with him. Was she falling in love with him? No way! She wasn't. Why then she didn't give it back to him when he was rude? She didn't know. All she knew was– he was the same old man prejudiced with the same old school thoughts. They were in Mumbai for some work after which they will both go their own separate ways. That was it.

"What I meant was, you should seriously join an NGO or social organization or politics if you really want to make a difference in people's lives. I am with you. You can do that."

Rahim changed his tone and softened a great deal when he found her non-communicative. Ayesha smiled. She was happy that Rahim realized his mistake and tried correcting it. She hoped that he will not repeat it in the future.

CHAPTER 27

The plane landed. Iqbal was still sleeping. Shweta woke him up. He was drowsy.

"We have reached, Iqbal, get up." She insisted. Iqbal opened his eyes and saw the flight crew walking to the exit. He smiled. Mission accomplished. Everyone returned home alive and safe.

Azad and Mushtaq, Iqbal, Shweta, Crystal didn't alight. The air hostess knew who they were and had an idea about what they had gone through recently.

"Please wait for the security assistant Mr. Iqbal and Miss Crystal." The air hostess made an announcement.

"I told everyone something when you were fast asleep." Crystal whispered in front of Azad, Mushtaq, Iqbal and Shweta. *What did she say?* Iqbal had a question mark in his eyes. He was curious about what she shared with the others.

"They wouldn't say a word about Azad or anyone else. I told them that god had given him a second chance so anyone says anything about Azad's past life would go against god's will. God will definitely punish that person." Azad heard it.

He hugged her with tears in his eyes.

***

"We are at the Chhatrapati Shivaji Airport, waiting for Iqbal, Crystal and everyone who was abducted by the terrorists …" Ayesha was reporting live for her television channel. Rahim held the camera for her.

Rahim and Ayesha were pushed around in the large crowd that had gathered to receive them. They weren't sure they will able to interview Iqbal.

Finally, Iqbal appeared with Crystal. The reporters were going crazy. As he appeared, they started clicking his pictures with Crystal.

Azad was standing silently with a racing heart. For him all this was a novelty, but it just a beginning. A new life had kicked off. He was standing with people he had fought against. Mushtaq, Tipu, Salim and Omar also stood beside him anxiously.

There was a barrage of questions from the reporters. Iqbal calmly informed them that he and the entire unit was exhausted.

He would do a media conference soon. The reporters were rubbing shoulders and cameras and struggling to click pictures and shoot videos so that they can telecast it live. They kept asking questions, Iqbal and Crystal ignored them and left.

Crystal's car was ready with personal security.

Azad met Crystal the star, for the first time. He saw the public going crazy for her. Her security in uniform, had her covered fully, in spite of it they were finding it difficult to control the crowd. The crowd was cheering "Crystal, Crystal". Media kept begging for a photo or a word from her.

Crystal invited Iqbal, Mushtaq and others home. "Meet me at my residence." She held Azad's hand and pulled him. Azad was pleasantly surprised with her actions and hopped into her car. He looked at her face. She looked back.

"What?" Crystal asked.

"Nothing" Azad smiled.

Azad and Crystal settled in her black SUV. The driver moved it out carefully navigating the surrounding crowd. Two security cars were covering Crystal 's SUV.

***

Prabhas Venkatesh heard the news. His manager Disha Sharma wanted to discuss it when he was back from his shoot. He had already given dates to another project.

"We have hardly any dates left for Iqbal." Disha was skeptical.

"Iqbal's project is important. He would like to finish it ASAP. It's hyped." Prabhas hinted that she had to pursue Iqbal.

"If it is made and released on time– it could be a blockbuster." Prabhas Venkatesh added, "Iqbal is good film maker."

"They need us more than we need them," Disha was smart, "We would renegotiate the contract for remuneration with fresh dates." Disha knew how to milk the project.

"Yes, let them call us." Prabhas Venkatesh lit a cigarette, "Has Iqbal called?"

"His flight just landed." Disha informed, "Crystal and Iqbal were the *breaking news* tonight. All news channels covered them."

"Journalists contacted me too." Prabhas Venkatesh didn't like that part of conversation, "I refused to talk on this issue. I mean who the hell is interested in talking on these controversial issues."

"Yeah, it makes no sense." Disha supported the star.

CHAPTER 28

Mumbai

Crystal's SUV hit the roads of Mumbai. Crystal looked at Azad.

Azad was quiet. He didn't know what to expect next. His life was in the hands of others; as others' lives were in his hands earlier. The tables had turned.

He had to wait and watch. *What was to happen to him? What kind of music will he face tomorrow?* Azad was left with just question marks only time had answers to. All he could do was to hold on to the faith he had in his Allah.

Crystal was still holding his hand– it meant a lot to him. Azad looked out. The city was brightly lit. Big flyovers, high raised buildings, and sea side. He was amazed by the Worli sea face bridge when the car reached Bandra.

The car stopped in front of a white bungalow.

***

Priyanka Singh, Crystal's manager was waiting for her anxiously.

She hugged her warmly and looked relieved. Priyanka looked at Azad.

"Who is this handsome?" she whispered.

"He is Beb." Crystal introduced Azad, "He is my friend. We call him Azad."

Azad smiled and looked at her. Priyanka shook hands and smiled back.

"Good evening madam." Raghu and Nandan welcomed her.

"Hello! All well?"

"Yes mam! How are you?" Raghu asked, "What happened to that terrorist Jabbar Ellahi? We saw his video. He was so deadly. I was scared when he said that he would kill everyone."

Crystal looked at him.

"Can we have coffee Raghu?" Crystal wanted them to stop that conversation. Azad's face had turned red.

"You started your nonsense again." Priyanka too got upset. Both of them went to the kitchen.

"Call Iqbal. Ask him where he has reached. We have an urgent meeting with the crew." Crystal instructed Priyanka.

"Now?"

"Yes." Crystal told her without looking at her, "We have a press conference tomorrow."

***

Crystal took Azad into her lavish house. He looked down to see his reflection in the shining white floor. Her bungalow was spacious and full of antique stuff – almost like a museum.

"Washroom! Take a shower Azad, Iqbal will be here soon." She said and went inside. Azad stood alone quietly, soaking the environment. Priyanka was busy making calls.

Crystal came out with some clothes and a bathrobe. Azad took it and went in the direction Crystal pointed, to the washroom. He wanted to be alone for some time. He felt good.

He stood in front of a full-length mirror and looked at his own reflection. The guy staring back at him was not a terrorist but an actor. His life had changed so much, so quickly! He had not run to catch it but it just transformed –like a butterfly breaking out of a cocoon. Crystal was there supporting him through this transformational journey.

He stood under the warm shower– his past life was being washed off him.

***

1:35 AM

Azad changed into the clothes Crystal had handed him, beige lowers and a round neck yellow T-shirt. He looked smashing. Crystal too had a shower and got into clean white shorts and a maroon sleeveless top. She looked sexy.

Crystal looked at him and smiled. Both got in to the conference room where normally Crystal took narrations and held business meetings with producers and directors.

Crystal 's bungalow got crowded in no time.

Priyanka was busy managing everyone.

She had no idea why Crystal had called them. Iqbal and Crystal had a long conversation inside the conference room with Mushtaq, Azad and Salim.

"Don't worry about accommodation." Crystal assured Iqbal.

"We are thirty of us." Mushtaq informed.

"Mushtaq, Salim and Omar will work as Azad's staff." Iqbal proposed, "We should be on the same page when we talk to anyone else." He waited and looked for their nods.

"We don't know anything about movie making." Omar sounded lost and worried.

"It is not rocket science– you will learn everything. I will teach you." Mushtaq said immediately, "We will manage Bhai's work. For me he was Bhai then, Bhai now. I will always be with him."

"What about the rest?" Salim asked.

"They will help Kabir in production." Shweta proposed.

"They can stay in my Goregaon flat." Crystal offered, "It is empty anyway."

"We have to make our IDs, Aadhar and other documents." Mushtaq was sharp, he knew what was needed the most.

"Hmm. I know someone, who will get it done." Kabir said.

The meeting went on till 4:30 AM.

When everyone was leaving, Crystal suddenly called Iqbal as he was about to hop in his car.

"What about Prabhas Venkatesh?" Crystal whispered.

"What about him?" Iqbal smiled, "We have our hero."

"Great! Announce Azad's name." Crystal supported.

***

Everyone left and Azad was left alone with Crystal.

Crystal showed Azad his bedroom and told him to make himself comfortable.

"I am sure you would like to sleep alone tonight." Crystal said naughtily. Azad blushed in response. Crystal went to her bedroom. Azad was alone. He stood in front of the window and looked out in the vast openness. He smelt the sea and could hear the crashing waves.

For Azad, everything seemed like a dream. Twenty-four hours earlier, he was a freedom fighter for his people, terrorist for rest of the world. His destiny took a turn and he found himself in a completely strange world. Whatever happened was Allah's wish. He accepted his wish. He thanked Allah. He didn't realize when he slept.

***

Iqbal came home and crashed. He had a media conference that day at 2:00 PM.

***

Srinagar police station at 7:00 AM.

Javed Khan's phone rang non-stop. He talked to sub inspector Mahip Jadda.

"There were four murders reported from Shabbir Mallik's bungalow. Please come as soon as possible."

The police recovered four dead bodies for Panchnama.

Shabbir Mallik, Muneer Ahmed Lone, Luckman and Liyakat Khan.

Someone had killed them the previous night. Javed saw the pools of blood caked maroon on the carpet and the white marble floor. *One who plays with fire gets burnt at the end of the day.*

Shabbir was a big leader of Kashmir. A huge crowd gathered around his house. They whispered among themselves but no one came forward to speak. No one had heard any sounds.

"It seems that they were killed last night." Mahip Jadda guessed.

Javed was pensive, he called Aditya Raghuvanshi and reported the killings.

Aditya heard it. *Why was Shabbir killed?* He brainstormed, something was not quite fitting the whole puzzle. *Was Iqbal hiding something? Was he?*

***

Bandstand, Mumbai.

Azad got up and saw a very beautiful girl waking him up. For a moment he thought he was in paradise. It was none other than Crystal. She had a tray in her hand.

"Did you sleep well? Do you want to sleep some more?" She asked touching his forehead to check whether he was alright. Azad's Ammi touched him like that when he was a kid. Crystal kissed him on the lips. He kissed her back. She climbed in to bed and hugged him tight.

"Your hand has a magical touch." Azad was moved. He welled.

"Magical touch made you cry?" Crystal joked to ease him, "Did you sleep well?"

"I have no idea how long I slept. I was dead to the world. I opened my eyes and thought I was in paradise when I saw you. It took me some time to recognize you." Azad got up and said.

"Do you recognize me now my blue-eyed boy?" Crystal joked.

"Perhaps …"

"What would you like to have- tea, coffee or weed Sir?" Crystal was in a mood to please him and make him feel at home.

"Weed?" Azad was surprised, "Here?"

"Yes Sir, here." Crystal smiled, "I got it for you."

Azad hugged her. Crystal offered him a joint.

Azad picked it up and lit it. He pulled a couple of drags and passed it to Crystal. They enjoyed smoking together.

"It is noon." She said, "We have to hurry. We have a press conference this afternoon."

"We?" he was surprised.

"We will announce that you are doing *Azadi* as a hero and not Prabhas Venkatesh."

***

Iqbal woke up to the call bell ringing relentlessly. He opened the door and found Lalwani standing at the door.

"Time to get up my star director." Lalwani knew Iqbal was the only director who got famous without making any movie.

"I called Disha and Prabhas Venkatesh." Lalwani told him, "His dates are a big problem. I want this film to be made and released ASAP. Hit while the iron is hot!"

"Don't worry I have got a solution." Iqbal got up and headed to the kitchen "Would you like to have tea or coffee?"

"Nothing for me," Lalwani just wanted to discuss the film project *Azadi*, "You have no idea. They are asking for double the money for dates now!"

"I will call them right now." Iqbal called Prabhas.

Disha picked up the call instead of Prabhas Venkatesh.

"Hi Iqbal. How are you?" Disha sounded cold. She knew they would talk about Prabhas Venkatesh's dates.

"We are back and wanted to start shooting ASAP so that we can…" Disha interjected, "Dates are an issue Iqbal. Prabhas has given dates to Anurag Kashyap– you know he is doing great nowadays."

"Oh …" Iqbal showed concern, "But we have to finish the shoot as quickly as possible."

"We have to revise the entire contract as far as the cost is concerned." Disha stated the real issue.

"Mr. Lalwani will take that call." Iqbal suggested looking at Lalwani.

"Talk to him and let me know." She said and disconnected the call.

Iqbal knew this was inevitable.

"She disconnected the line." Iqbal said sipping tea, "Prabhas would charge us double now–you were right!"

"We have to negotiate and bring the cost down," Lalwani was not happy.

Iqbal looked at him and smiled, "It's not money. It's the dates. Prabhas has committed dates to Anurag Kashyap. He has started shooting. Anurag is a tough guy. They can't say no to him."

"What is the way out?"

"Our film is hyped and we need no star." Iqbal looked into Lalwani's eyes and struck the blow, "I have shot with someone. I will show you the footage." Iqbal said and connected the hard disc with the laptop and showed him Azad's shooting.

"He is good. Who is this young man? What a screen presence. He is star material!" Lalwani was impressed, "But on one condition, he is a new comer so payment…"

"Don't worry, payment is not a problem. He will be happy to take whatever you give him." Iqbal pacified him.

"What about her?"

"Crystal?" Iqbal guessed.

"Yes, will she agree to work with a new comer?" Lalwani had his doubts.

"Azad is her friend." Iqbal smiled, "Crystal recommended him."

Iqbal put Lalwani at ease.

Lalwani calculated. He was making a movie in less than half the cost as compared to what he had budgeted for earlier. The biggest component was the huge fees of the superhero Prabhas. He knew the movie had been hyped. It will rock. This movie could even cross one hundred million he assumed.

***

Iqbal announced Azad as the lead man in the press conference.

"He is Azad. He is our hero of *Azadi*." Iqbal introduced Azad. Cameras turned towards Azad and flashed away, "Azad look here. Sir, please see this side." Azad followed their request and smiled for the cameras. Crystal stood beside him and posed as his heroine.

"What happened to Prabhas Venkatesh?" Rahim asked.

"Unfortunately, he allotted his dated to another project."

"You are ready to work with a new comer like Azad?" Ayesha asked.

"I was a new comer once. He is a talented, handsome blue-eyed boy." Crystal replied.

"Mr. Azad where are you from?" one of the journalists asked.

"Let me introduce Azad," Iqbal took over immediately. He knew Azad couldn't handle it right now, "Azad is from London. He has done theatre. He was in touch. He came with us as a crew member to see and learn movie making. He too was abducted along with us." Iqbal briefed.

"How do you feel Mr. Azad?" another journalist asked.

"Say *I feel great*." Crystal whispered in his ear.

"I feel great." Azad parroted.

Rahim was noticing him, "Something is not right." He said to Ayesha.

***

All the leading newspapers carried the story on page 3, 'Azad, the blue-eyed boy becomes the lead actor of Iqbal's *Azadi*.' Aditya read the news.

Aditya Raghuvanshi and Javed Khan were still not sure of what actually happened during the operation. "Have you seen the video of Jabbar Ellahi? He too had blue eyes."

"Yesterday we conducted the operation. Ten terrorists killed, Rehman and his two men killed and Shabbir and his three men murdered." Aditya was trying to figure out, "These killings were all linked."

"Of course they were!" Javed was on the same page.

Something was fishy. Why did Iqbal change the hero? Prabhas Venkatesh to Azad? Who was Azad? Aditya and Javed brainstormed all possibilities and every possible angle. They wanted to get to the root of the mystery behind murders that took place last night in Srinagar.

Rehman and Shabbir were dead. It was done systemically. No one was alive to tell who exactly Jabbar Ellahi was. What did he look like? Aditya knew it was a well-planned action to fool everybody. Jabbar Ellahi was still alive.

***

Aditya and Javed both were appreciated for their tremendously successful operation. They would be surely awarded some medal. They expected a promotion plus a medal on 26 January! General recommended their names. But Aditya wasn't happy.

***

Ajit Dayal visited the army camp to meet up with Jang Bahadur. He saw Aditya Raghuvanshi while leaving the military camp. He called his name. Aditya stopped and walked up to him.

"Tea?" Ajit offered.

"Sure sir."

Both had tea and snacks in the lavish army canteen.

Aditya shared his concern.

"I think Jabbar Ellahi is still alive. We need to investigate the matter and unearth the truth."

Ajit was surprised, but he sipped the tea and looked at the beautiful valley.

"Iqbal told us Jabbar Ellahi was no one but an idea- the boss."

"That is something I am not fully convinced about."

"You mean to say Iqbal lied to us." Ajit wasn't sure.

"Iqbal has not told us the whole truth. There was some tacit understanding between the terrorists and Iqbal. Though what and more importantly, why– I can't figure out."

"Have you shared this with anyone?"

"Not yet sir."

"Hmm." Ajit asked a straight question, "Do you want to investigate it further?"

"Yes sir!" Aditya had shared important information, "I need to go to Mumbai for this."

"Keep it a secret. I will talk to your seniors." Ajit was smart enough to handle such situations. He was the mind behind revocation of Article 370 in Kashmir. He knew how to make things work. He was in touch with everyone directly so that he has his fingers on the pulse.

"Report to me directly." He said approving his investigation.

Aditya knew politics was complicated.

Aditya left for Mumbai immediately.

***

Ajit met Rudra Shekhar and asked him to investigate for him. The investigation was regarding Iqbal and his team. He wanted Shekhar to publish the information. Rahim got a call to dig out all the information about the film crew.

"Find out details of all the movie crew members." Shekhar put him on a new job, "Attend the shoot every day. Tell me what is happening. We are starting a bulletin about *Azadi*– a daily shooting report." Shekhar moved his cards smartly as Ajit Dayal had told him to keep it a secret and keep him abreast. Ajit wanted to know if the two versions (Aditya's version and reporter's version) were matching or not.

"If you find anything fishy, tell me immediately," instructed Shekhar

"What do you doubt? Who do you doubt?" Rahim was curious to know.

"Watch Iqbal and his entire crew."

"Okay." Rahim didn't argue with him. He was enjoying his time with Ayesha.

***

Prabhas Venkatesh was pissed off when he came to know that Iqbal had chosen someone else and his plan had failed. *I have been replaced by a newcomer? How dare he?*

He called Crystal asking her to quit Iqbal's movie.

"I suggest you should also take a call to …", He paused. "It's up to you. I am doing a movie with Sanjay Bhansali. I have already recommended your name for the role opposite me." Prabhas lured Crystal, "I hope you are wise. You are such a big star. Why should you work with an unknown actor? Who knows him?"

Prabhas was confident that she would quit the film. Especially after he called and requested her.

Crystal though it was inevitable. Prabhas was desperate and felt insulted. Iqbal's *Azadi* was the talk of the town. She knew the movie had media's attention. News was flashing every day.

"Do you want me to talk to Iqbal?" Crystal offered. She didn't want to antagonize Prabhas.

"I have no problem with Iqbal. We are a part of the same big family of movie fraternity. South Indian film industry and Bollywood have become one and are working together. No one knew him when Iqbal came with Lalwani. Today he is popular, but his film is yet to be made and released." Prabhas expressed his concern, he didn't want to miss the movie. Crystal could get him back in the movie he thought.

"I think Iqbal isn't making the decision. Let me talk to him." Crystal defended Iqbal.

Prabhas decided not to wait. He called Disha immediately and put her to task, "Initiate the talk with Lalwani and Iqbal. Try all your sources. I don't want to miss the movie."

Disha understood that the situation was grave and it had to be dealt carefully. She was confident. Iqbal would replace Azad once she allotted the dates to him.

***

Iqbal planned everything on a war footing. He worked 24x7. He made a set in Film City and started shooting with Azad. The crew worked double shifts.

Prabhas was shocked when Iqbal said he is busy shooting his movie. Iqbal promised to do the next film with Prabhas. He was committed to Azad as he had already announced him as the hero in the press conference. He pretended that it was Lalwani's decision– not his.

"Unbelievable!" Prabhas blamed Disha and fired her. She had managed his business for over seven years.

***

Azad worked hard too. He took up the challenge to complete the movie. The post production started simultaneously. Iqbal made it sync sound so that no dubbing was required.

The edit was done on the set. Iqbal used to take a final call on the edit after the shooting was over, on a daily basis. While going back after the shoot he planned his next schedule. The movie released in a record time of twenty-five days.

The PR was done aggressively. Iqbal knew public memory was short. He kept sending information about the film on print, electronic and social media. The trailer of the movie was launched within a week's time.

The publicity began. Azad, Iqbal Crystal traveled to Delhi, Pune, Ghaziabad, Lucknow and many other big and small towns. Azad proved to be a quick learner and spoke in front of the media fearlessly. His posters were everywhere. He was posing with Crystal on big hoardings all over the metro cities.

***

Aditya Raghuvanshi met the crew members and tried to find out who Azad was. He got no new clues. He met Prabhas who was anyway upset with Iqbal.

Both met over a drink.

"Who is this new guy?"

"No idea, some joker who doesn't know what performance is."

"Why did Iqbal take a new guy?"

"It wasn't him, it's Lalwani"

"Who is Lalwani?"

"Iqbal's investor and producer, he is one of the richest investors in Bollywood."

"But you are a star, why did they replace you?"

Prabhas smiled. "I am expensive, Lalwani might have thought hiring a newcomer would benefit him. They don't pay a newcomer and finish the movie fast. People will soon forget about the abduction news, so Iqbal and the team had to wrap it all up fast. They are making a big mistake, people want to watch a star perform. The movie will bomb no matter how hyped it is. The movie doesn't run on hype or publicity! A star assures box office collection." Prabhas sipped his single malt scotch, "They have made a bad choice, audience will reject the film in the very first show. Next show no one will watch, it will be a …" he was drunk, he fumbled.

"Flop film…" Aditya completed it.

"Not only flop but a total wash-out, disastrous movie. Audience will not watch the next show. Iqbal will come running to me regretting his decision. But it is not his fault, he is a new director. It is all Lalwani."

"But you have no idea who this new actor is?" Aditya was not really interested in Iqbal's movie. His interest was in Azad. He thought Prabhas might have some information about him.

"Nobody has any idea about him. He will vanish after one film. Who cares who he is? He is a nobody and will be nobody." Prabhas pronounced the verdict.

***

Iqbal proved everyone wrong who predicted the movie wouldn't work at the box office.

The movie was a massive hit when it was released.

Iqbal's hard work paid off. His first film was a huge hit.

Azad was a star overnight.

Lalwani threw a massive party and called everyone including Prabhas Venkatesh. He turned up graciously and congratulated Iqbal.

CHAPTER 29

Rahim didn't find anything suspicious about Azad, except that there was a big gossip about Crystal having an affair with Azad. It happened in every movie– the grapevine paired the hero and the heroin. It gave the film additional publicity.

***

Rahim and Ayesha were back from Mumbai. Rudra Shekhar was happy. They did well.

"I have a question Rahim." Shekhar smiled.

"Shoot."

"You are a serious reporter. You didn't want to report Bollywood. You hated that job. But this time, you didn't crib and thoroughly reported the film industry. How come?" He asked.

"It was a political story which turned in to a Bollywood story." Rahim replied.

Shekhar was not convinced. *When Rahim hated Bollywood how come he worked for so long on this project? Did he like being with Ayesha?*

Rahim was awake that night and thought about the question Shekhar had thrown at him. *Was it because of Ayesha?* They had decided to stay in one flat in Mumbai to save money.

"It would be economical" Ayesha proposed and he agreed. They shifted in a small but decent apartment in Andheri west. They lived together, reported together. They shared every moment. Those moments made for happy memories for Rahim. He missed Ayesha when they returned to Srinagar.

Rahim got a message from Ayesha, inviting him to watch *Azadi*.

"I am going to watch it. Would you like to join me?"

"Yes, why not? Which show?"

Both watched *Azadi* together sharing popcorn in the theatre. They come out from the auditorium and stood facing each other.

"I was thinking if we could work together."

"We already work together. We both report for the same Valley news. Isn't it?"

"Yes, I thought maybe work on the same project." Rahim tried to be clearer.

"How? You report politics and crime —my section is entertainment. Do you want to change your area of interest?" Ayesha knew Rahim loved her, but was hesitant to express it.

"I will speak to Shekhar about you, do you want to come in crime and politics reporting?"

"No" Ayesha gave a straight reply. Rahim was offended and confused. She called him for a movie, they shared the popcorn and now– why she was talking so rudely?

"You always wanted to report crime and politics, didn't you?"

"Why do you want to drag me in crime reporting now? Why are you suddenly interested in my interests?"

"Just like that."

"If I ask you to buy a drink for me where would you take me?" Ayesha changed the topic.

Rahim knew Ayesha was beyond his reach. She was an independent girl living a free life.

"Mughal Darbar." Rahim replied calmly.

They reached Mughal Darbar. Ayesha placed the order for both of them. They had dinner and chatted till late night.

CHAPTER 30

Iqbal was relaxed after the massive success of his first movie. Azad became a mega star. Lalwani was the happiest man on the planet. He made twenty million US dollars worldwide with *Azadi*.

Two months just zipped past. Iqbal was ready to make *Azadi 2*. The first rough draft was almost ready. Lalwani was more than willing to back the movie up. Iqbal wanted to brief Azad and discuss the possible shooting dates.

Azad and Mushtaq were not taking Iqbal's phone calls. Shweta too tried calling them.

Iqbal called Crystal and came to know that he had shifted to a new apartment with Mushtaq, Tipu, Salim and Omar.

"Media, you know, started gossiping about Azad and me." Crystal explained the reason why Azad shifted from her bungalow to a new apartment in Andheri west.

Iqbal and Shweta decided to meet Azad at his residence. They went to Azad's new apartment in Andheri west. The lift took them to the terrace apartment on the 29 floor.

They came out of the lift and found a man standing in all white– white trousers, white shirt, white shoes and black goggles– waiting for the lift.

Iqbal glanced at him and asked, "29 A?" He asked the man.

"Yes." He was hoping they would recognize him.

But Iqbal and Shweta were in hurry. They went ahead to ring the doorbell. The man in white came close, smiled and said, "Hello big director! Don't you recognize me?"

Iqbal turned back and finally recognized Mushtaq.

"Oh, it's you Mushtaq! Why didn't you take my calls? Both of us have been trying to get in touch with you." Iqbal complained angrily. Iqbal and Shweta were quite amused when they saw Mushtaq.

"I was busy." Mushtaq's reply was short and abrupt. Iqbal looked at him. He certainly was a changed man.

"May I ask you something Iqbal?" Mushtaq looked at Iqbal. Iqbal didn't say anything, just looked at him quietly. Mushtaq took his silence as a go ahead and continued, "Azad Bhai's last movie was a massive hit, right? Where is his remuneration? Have you paid us, so that we could also survive Iqbal?"

Mushtaq sighed, "I am his manager. I have to take care of many guys you know! I have to pay installments of car and flat. Bhai is busy all the time."

"But I called you to discuss money. You know the situation at that time. We had to hurry up everything. I am making the next movie *Azadi - 2*, I need to know the available dates." Iqbal put forth the proposal.

"Forget the dates, you have no idea how busy Bhai is." Mushtaq refused flatly, "You know how many films he has signed? All top studios have signed him, RSVP, VIACOM, Excel, Dharma, Red Chilies, Fox Star, Mukta Arts –You name a studio and they have signed him. He is doing double shift –day and night. All top directors want to work with him. Yesterday, you know who came here?" Mushtaq took a pause and looked at Iqbal.

"Who?" Shweta's interest piqued.

"James Cameroon." He was here to sign Bhai up for a project.

"Oh really! Did he sign him." Shweta asked sarcastically. She knew he was lying. If James was in Mumbai, media would report.

"We said no."

"You said no to James Cameroon?" Iqbal faked surprise; he knew Mushtaq was lying.

"Why?" Shweta faked concern.

"Date problems." Mushtaq replied in no time, "Bhai is booked for four years."

Both Shweta and Iqbal looked at each other. They knew Mushtaq was turning their proposal down. They were flabbergasted and didn't know what to do.

"I have to leave; my girlfriend is waiting. I have a date today."

Mushtaq said suddenly stepping towards the lift.

"Who are you dating, Chandni?"

"I broke up with her." Mushtaq was quick, "I am dating Kangana."

"Kangana who?" Shweta asked.

"Kangana Ranauat" Mushtaq replied coolly.

"Chandni moved on with Omar. She is not my type of girl. Kangana is." Mushtaq concluded.

They couldn't believe he was the same Mushtaq.

"Where is Azad Bhai?" Iqbal asked

"He is with *Bhabhijaan* (sister-in-law)." Came a quick reply.

"Who is *Bhabhijaan*?"

"You forgot Crystal *Bhabhijaan*." Mushtaq pressed the lift button. He wanted to leave.

"We made him Azad. Don't forget that." Shweta couldn't stop herself any longer.

Mushtaq heard it.

"What did you say?" Mushtaq didn't like Shweta's tone.

"You heard it." Shweta was worked up.

"You know because of whom you are standing here alive today?"

"Go ahead I am listening." Shweta provoked him.

"Because of me. Have you forgotten everything? Or should I remind you? Who had not loaded the gun? Me. Who suggested Azad Bhai that Allah wanted this? This was all Allah's wish. If not for me, all of you would have been dead. He would have killed all 370 in one go. Do not forget all that happened, happened because of me. I planned everything." Mushtaq had grown too big for his boots.

"Unbelievable!" Shweta was shocked at how Mushtaq twisted and turned facts and took credit for everything.

The lift door opened and Azad walked out of the lift with Crystal.

"Iqbal." Azad hugged him, "How are you my brother?"

Crystal hugged Shweta and Iqbal warmly.

"We have been calling you to meet you today." Crystal complained, "Check your phone.".

Iqbal saw missed calls from Crystal. His phone was on silent.

"Please come in, why are you standing here?" Azad said and looked at Mushtaq, "Why are they standing out here?" Azad was a little upset.

"I told them to come inside and wait for Bhai but they wanted to rush to meet someone important." Mushtaq lied blatantly, "Please come in Iqbal." Omar opened the door.

They went in and parked themselves on the comfy Italian sofa. The new apartment was big. Crystal had designed it, so it was done up tastefully– not too extravagant but classy.

"I heard James was here," Shweta wanted to expose Mushtaq's lie. She deliberately took up that topic.

"Who James?" Azad asked.

"The international director James Cameroon!"

"Why would he be here?" Azad was surprised.

Shweta smiled at Mushtaq. Mushtaq was embarrassed.

He changed the topic, "What would you like– wine? Vodka? Champagne?"

"We are good. Thank you," Iqbal smiled, "I am planning to make *Azadi*- 2."

"Tell me one thing Iqbal. Do you always talk shop? Have something first. Let's talk about your marriage. When are you two getting married?" Azad asked and turned towards Mushtaq, "Ask someone to make drinks for all of us. Let's celebrate."

"Yes Boss." He said and called Omar to arrange for the drinks.

"Yes, he always talks work and films. You should take a break Iqbal. How is your romantic life?" Crystal agreed with Azad.

Azad was looking graceful, his face glowed. The fame and money both suited him well. Azad was happy.

"You are right. I was telling him to come in – have a drink and chill but he asked me only professional questions. Not good Iqbal. We are friends too." Mushtaq pulled Iqbal's leg.

"Let's celebrate the meeting of great friends!" Crystal cheered.

"And don't worry. No dates issue for you. I am a star today because of you," Azad assured him, "I would love to work with you again."

***

Iqbal, Shweta, Crystal and Azad cracked jokes and laughed a lot. They recalled the time they spent, when they shot the first romantic scene with Crystal and Azad.

Mushtaq's phone rang. Everyone heard the funny ring tone (An old English song)-

'Tell me if you love me,

And so how am I ever to know?

You always tell me -

Perhaps, perhaps, perhaps…'

Mushtaq took the call. After he ended the call, he started dancing funnily.

"He has gone mad." Shweta commented.

"You too will go mad when you hear the news. Bhai got a national award."

The news stunned everyone. They hugged and congratulated one another. Later when Iqbal checked his phone, he had received the message about the award. Iqbal as a director and Azad as a debut actor had both won the national award.

They partied till midnight.

CHAPTER 31

Iqbal was on cloud nine when he got back home with Shweta.

He finally got the acknowledgement he deserved after years of hard work. Shweta was always with him. "This wasn't possible without your support."

Shweta was moved to tears when Iqbal said that.

They heard the doorbell ring. They wanted to be alone for some time. *Who had come at this hour? Must be his friends- to congratulate and celebrate. The news of Iqbal's national award must have gone viral.* Shweta opened the door. They were surprised to see Aditya Raghuvanshi standing at the door.

"What a pleasant surprise! Please come in." Iqbal welcomed him. Aditya entered. He sat and looked around. Shweta served him water and sweets.

"Our movie has got two national awards– best director and debut actor award." Shweta shared the good news. Aditya was silent. Iqbal guessed he wanted to say something.

"Congratulations!" He shook hands with Iqbal.

"Iqbal you are a good director, you worked hard and are successful today. Do you want to share any secret with me?" Aditya suddenly changed the topic and said seriously.

"My life is an open book. I have nothing to hide." Iqbal guessed Aditya's intent. *Did he find out about Azad? How? Or was he just shooting in the dark?*

"Who is Azad?" Aditya asked directly. Iqbal's face paled.

"Azad is our lead actor of *Azadi*. And today, an award-winning movie star."

"I am not a fool Iqbal. He is a terrorist, a murderer. He killed Shabbir Mallik and Muneer Lone along with two others working for Shabbir– the same night he left for Mumbai." Aditya bombarded him with the facts known to him, "He murdered them before he came to Mumbai."

"What a joke. A murderer becomes a star." Iqbal laughed at him.

"Yes, you made this joke a reality. I saw the movie *Azadi* and tried to remember where I have seen him. His face was spinning in front of me after I went home. Then I suddenly remembered I saw him with you during the operation. I remember you took out the jeep from the ditch. He was sitting beside you. I fired at him, but the bullet didn't hit him. You saved him. Why? Reasons are best known to you."

"The bullet you fired, hit me. I could have died." Iqbal said.

"You are alive, not dead Iqbal." Aditya was angry and rude, "Don't evade my question."

"So, when you saw me and the terrorist what did you see? A man looked like Azad in that frame of mind and from that distance? Really? Having a gun in hand, firing at terrorists you noticed his face– are you serious Aditya? Hadn't you seen they had beaten me brutally, my head was bleeding, there was a bandage on my head" Iqbal sighed and continued, "According to you the man who kidnapped me, thrashed me and threatened to kill us all– I have given him a chance to be a hero in my movie? Is this what your investigation says? He is a professional actor, not a terrorist. People loved his performance. He is a star today. I am sorry if you think that, no one would buy this."

"That is my finding and this man has no previous records. Who he was? Where did he come from– London or Dubai?

"It's in the public domain, see Wikipedia, he is from Dubai and was doing theatre in London."

"He has no record in London. I have checked with many theatre groups."

"He wasn't famous. He did theatre for a few months with some small-time group and came to Mumbai to become an actor."

"Hmm, you are a story writer." Aditya smiled cunningly.

Iqbal didn't say a word after that. He knew he was upset. Shweta was quiet. Aditya continued talking, "I also checked the guest list with hotel India Pride at Srinagar. They had a record of 371 persons staying at the hotel. Their identity cards were in the system. There was no one called Azad. He appeared out of nowhere."

"Many came on the second day of the shooting. Azad was one of them. They came straight to the shooting location and they were supposed to check in to the hotel after the pack up. But in the meantime, we were abducted." Shweta justified, "That's the reason there was no entry in the hotel register."

"Okay. Do you know the voices of Azad and Jabbar in the video match perfectly?" Aditya threw another bombshell– this was a strong one. He was sure Iqbal couldn't deny the fact.

"Do you know that two voices match exactly in a million people." Iqbal defused the bomb, "It is just a coincidence that voice of Jabbar and Azad is the same."

"Okay, the masked video of the terrorist Jabbar Ellahi –have you seen that video? The eyes? Jabbar had blue eyes, same as Azad."

"They recoded the threatening message, it happened in front of our eyes, there were two different persons - one faced the camera with the mask, another read the message which was written. It seemed like one single guy but in reality, there were two people involved in sending the threatening message." Iqbal explained with confidence.

Aditya raised his voice, "I am not buying that. You are a traitor. Movie star Azad was Jabbar who killed many innocent people. He will kill again. Once a terrorist, always a terrorist. They have motives you wouldn't know. He is posing as an artist but he would plan one day to destroy the Mumbai city. You will regret that day." Aditya spewed his thoughts.

"You know what is the problem of our society?" Iqbal asked coolly.

"Yes, you will say we don't trust Muslims, right?" Aditya drew a conclusion of his own.

"No, you are wrong here too. In our society, film makers who actually show the way of life have zero importance. We make this society. People copy us and inculcate in their lives what we show through our films. Films are mirrors. People see their good, bad, ugly faces and react. Do you have any idea how much time it takes to become a mirror? One has to melt himself for years." Iqbal sighed, "You think only you are responsible for saving the nation, because you are a soldier? We have no responsibility? Who saved the entire movie crew? Tell me honestly, were you able to save us? You had the army, police force and yet you couldn't do it. You call me a traitor? Please understand, unless we all make collective efforts it would be a half and paralyzed society which we are today. Divided at every level. Because its base is feudal."

"You are lecturing me?"

"Oh Yes! You don't like to listen to the facts of life. You have a habit of listening to blood sucking politicians who kill people, lie to rule this great nation. Only if you are ready to listen sir. Azad is an artist busy in his movies." Iqbal mentioned. "Instead of sending an army– send a message of love to Kashmir's bleeding hearts. Heal it."

Shweta spoke, "Do you know something? Would you like some data? In this country more Dalits die cleaning the gutters than soldiers die on the borders. We pay respect to them who die fighting for the nation. Do we even pay attention to Dalits who clean our roads, stations, carry our garbage every morning? We do not." Shweta was unstoppable today, "That is also a form of terrorism– keep the poor deprived in the name of cast and religion."

"Would you like to have tea or coffee?" Iqbal needed it badly now. He went in the kitchen. Shweta continued, "You came all the way from Kashmir to Mumbai to find this out? I advise you to travel and see what is happening in this country."

"Tell me, was he Jabbar Ellahi? Did you change his name?"

"Yes, of course we changed his name. Azad was the protagonist in the film." she paused, "His name was Amir Hussain earlier and not Jabbar Ellahi." Shweta clarified.

Iqbal came with a tray and served them tea.

"My investigation says he was Jabbar Ellahi." Aditya sipped his tea.

Aditya kept the cup on the table after finishing the last sip.

"Thank you for the tea. I will expose everyone on the day he goes to Delhi to take the national award." he said, then he got up and left as coolly.

Shweta and Iqbal looked at each other. Tension built.

"How did he know?" Shweta asked.

"He is guessing. He doesn't know. And even if he knows he can't prove anything. The media will start guessing but at the end of the day nothing will be proved." Iqbal himself was worried when he said that. He wanted Shweta not to worry.

***

Iqbal knew that the army men were trained to see the world in black and white– right or wrong. For them people were friends or foes. They took orders and shot. They didn't ask who they were firing at. Or why? Whether they were innocent or guilty. They weren't allowed to think. They could have anything and everything– best of alcohol, best of medicines, all comforts. But at the time of action, they just followed their senior's orders. His school mate Mukesh was in the army who died fighting the terrorists on the border.

Mukesh used to tell Iqbal how they used to kill Kashmiris; sometimes they weren't terrorists but innocent people. They were stuck between terrorists and their conscience.

Even now they were stuck.

Iqbal stayed up smoking till morning while Shweta was fast asleep.

***

Rudra Shekhar called Rahim the moment he entered the office.

Ayesha was already in Shekhar's cabin. Both of them looked at him. Rahim found it fishy. *Why was she waiting for him? What was she doing there?*

"Come, Rahim, have a seat". Shekhar's voice was serious. He sank into the couch in a corner of the cabin. He didn't sit next to Ayesha. They both looked pretty serious and he waited for them to speak up.

"I have an assignment in Delhi. Would you like to go?"

"I don't mind."

"Would you like to take Ayesha with you?"

"She isn't interested in crime and politics."

"Hmm." Shekhar drank a glass of water and looked at Rahim, "*Azadi* has bagged two national awards."

"I know." Rahim knew the news.

"You have to cover that event with Ayesha." Shekhar took out two passes from the front drawer of his table. Rahim looked at it. He looked at Shekhar and Ayesha. They were smiling. Ayesha laughed looking him. He simply smiled.

"Coffee?" Shekhar asked.

"I am feeling hungry can I have something to eat?" Rahim demanded.

"Me too."

"Let's go to the canteen. You both take off for the day." Shekhar proposed.

Ayesha and Rahim made good use of the off day by shopping for appropriate attire for the award function. Both of them enjoyed shopping together.

***

Aditya Raghuvanshi looked through window of the plane headed to Delhi. The city of seven islands, Mumbai was visible from that height. The sea, shore line, high-rise buildings and slums. The metropolis had extreme destitute and prosperity, side by side. It had a place for everyone. Iqbal was one of them. Aditya had dug in to his past to establish if he had any links with the terrorists. Even Shweta was under scrutiny. Iqbal was squeaky clean, he did everything for his film. He had nothing to do with the terrorism or any plots and conspiracies. He was just an idiot, unaware of their deadly games. He cared only for his career as movie director. Azad had absolutely no past record in Mumbai. Iqbal had definitely lied about him. Iqbal would regret when Azad shows his true colors. He would plant bombs in the city.

Aditya had to perform his duties and save people's lives. He had suffered a lot when Jabbar Ellahi abducted the movie crew. He faced so much of humiliation at that time! Now it's time to expose Azad. He would be unmasked and Aditya would be the real hero. He would get his dues and get the name and fame he was entitled to! He smiled with such a pleasant day dream. Then he came back to the reality and looked at the beautiful air hostess.

"Can I have a coffee?"

"Cold or hot Sir?" she asked politely.

"A hot one."

The coffee was served. Major Aditya Raghuvanshi sipped his coffee and looked out through the window again. It was cloudy. Huge mattress of fluffy clouds was spread all around, some clouds were shining white but most were shades of gray.

CHAPTER 32

New Delhi. Raisina Hill. President auditorium.

Iqbal and his team were waiting for their names to be announced. The huge auditorium was packed with distinguished invitees. The stage was spacious. The president of India and information broadcasting minister Prakash Javadekar were the two dignitaries on the stage.

Iqbal and Azad were coached beforehand on their movements on the stage. They were instructed thoroughly on where to go, stand, receive the award and finally in which direction to exit. Iqbal and Azad were surprised to learn the discipline involved in receiving an award.

Ayesha and Rahim were covering the event with their camera team.

Azad and Crystal were happy. They saw Aditya Raghuvanshi enter the big auditorium. He sat down in a corner, quietly. Iqbal's anxiety levels went through the roof when he saw Aditya.

The announcement was made, "…And the best director award goes to Iqbal Ali for *Azadi*. We are also proud to call upon the stage Azad, for the best debut actor award for the same film." Azad went to the podium. Azad and Iqbal took the trophies.

The anchor asked Azad to speak a few words. Iqbal took Azad's trophy so that he would be more comfortable. Azad was a bit hesitant as he wasn't really prepared for a speech. Iqbal smiled and egged him on.

Azad stood beside Iqbal and took the mike.

"Do you know who I was? I wasn't Azad," Azad looked at the audience, turned his head to Iqbal. Iqbal had no idea what he was planning to say.

Aditya and Iqbal exchanged looks.

"I was Amir Hussain. Ammi gave me that name. I am now known as Azad." He paused, "Ammi used to tell me that I looked like a hero when I was a kid. She was right. She is not alive to see me today. I wish she could see me here, like this…" he paused.

"I wanted my audience to like me. But this shower of love and affection? People run to touch me. They are crazy to take a selfie with me. I am thankful to Allah for all this love. I think I am lucky, very lucky," Tears rolled down his cheek, "I thought I would become an actor and get some small parts in movies. Never in my wildest imagination I expected so much love from so many people. People treat me like an angle. They go mad when they see me, they shout out Beb, Blue-eyed boy …Crystal gave me that name," he looked at Crystal sitting in the front row. "This is my second birth. I was invisible in my previous life. Now people see me, adore me and follow me. I am overwhelmed with… so much love…? Ammi told me that my dreams would come true. She was right. She was so right." He looked at Iqbal. Everyone liked his candid speech. The audience was silently looking at him for more.

"What have I done? Just spoke writer's lines, obeyed director's instructions, wore costumes designed by another professional. And look at the magic! Audience knows me– not them. Audience loves me– not them. Seriously, we actors are blessed. I am blessed. I thank the 400 people who helped me be the star I am today and the audience. And Iqbal? I was 'nobody'– he made me Azad. Iqbal is no less than god for me. Writers and directors burn their lives to make others' lives. They are think-tanks. A country must respect film-makers, writers, authors and take their advice to build a nation. They are the soul of a nation. Iqbal not only made my life but taught me lesson in friendship."

"I appeal to the government to learn the same lesson and love people who protest and fight for freedom in Kashmir. Instead of sending army, spread love in Kashmir. Make friends with them and see how things change. The entire Kashmir will change. They will reciprocate with love. I guarantee."

The audience applauded for a full one minute.

Tears welled up in Aditya's eyes. He met Azad for the first time. When you get to know someone, make friends with them and try to understand them, things change. Aditya knew by now that Azad was not only harmless, but a wonderful person. He might have made mistakes and have had a bad past. He might have been a terrorist but today he wouldn't sacrifice the love he got from the people. He wouldn't take that risk. Never. He is a friend. All Kashmiris needed were friends– like him. Once that was done the Kashmir will have peace or else …

Iqbal and Azad were right. Instead of sending an army, send a message of love. He got up, walked down the aisle and went out of the auditorium.

The audience was clapping. Iqbal saw Aditya walking out of the auditorium. Crystal and Shweta wiped their tears and smiled through their tears.

Stories never end.

Abhik Bhanu (Published works)

A dark rainbow - 2013

The journey of life is easier for the normal, sighted people; thought Joy– a blind man. However, he realized that sight has its own limitations and that life without it might be far more enlightening. What blindness gives is a gift to look within. Those blessed with sight can be blind too if they lack a vision in life. He tumbled and stumbled on the rocky path of life to understand life's core and finally reached the ultimate truth that knowledge begins when one surrenders to ignorance. Admit that *I do not know!* A point where the mind is free from all collected burden and biases. The mind then becomes like a spotlessly clean mirror and reflects the ultimate knowledge of life. *A dark rainbow* is an honest effort to remove illusions of life and get to the ultimate truth through a roller coaster ride of life.

Stool pigeon – 2018

(Awarded the best book of the year by DadaSaheb Phalke Film Foundation – 2019)

Khabri, a stool pigeon, is a police informer who grew up on the streets of Dharavi slums in Mumbai. Thanks to his existence on the footpath he is privy to a lot of information. Nothing is ever lost to his keen eyes. Khabri is also a game-changer. Ria, the daughter of the police commissioner is diametrically opposite – **rich**, sophisticated girl with a free spirit and a heart of gold. These opposites attract each other after a chance encounter. A forbidden love between the ultra-polished and unpolished. *Stool pigeon* provides a bird's eye view on the destitute in India in an unfettered manner exposing the bare underbelly of the Indian socio-political ecosystem.

Blind faith - 2019

Blind faith is all about love and trust. Life is magical when you fall in love and live with a strong bond, in total harmony. The two of them trust each other completely as love is all about trust. Everything is lost when that trust is shattered. *Blind faith* touches the heart of the reader and forces one to sit back and think about love and forgiveness. Should one be forgiven? Or, let that person repent? Who suffers more– the one who was betrayed or the one who betrays? The author wants the readers to mull over relationships and possibility of holding it up. And what everything means at the end of the day. Read *Blind faith* to explore love and trust in difficult times.

Abhik Bhanu

Books in the pipeline
1. B @ the door – Thriller
2. English country – Classic.
3. X – Tokyo – Thriller
4. Dolphin – Murder Mystery
5. Ringmaster – Romance.
6. Mahatma after 150 years – Classic
www.abhikbhanu.net

Lightning Source UK Ltd.
Milton Keynes UK
UKHW010632301120
374362UK00001B/47

9 781649 085146